Decode Your Divorce

The Modern Law Handbook for Managing Your Divorce

THE ULTIMATE DIVORCE RESOURCE FOR ARIZONA FAMILY LAW

Decode Your Divorce

THE MODERN LAW HANDBOOK FOR MANAGING YOUR DIVORCE

BILLIE TARASCIO, JD

Table of Contents

Decode Your Divorce Introduction

Welcome! We are glad you are here. This book, written by Billie Tarascio at Modern Law, will answer some of the most common questions clients have about divorce and family law. This book will serve as your guide through the divorce process and help those who are representing themselves work with a roadmap, knowledge, and guidance.

Even if you are working with an attorney, it is likely you will have questions along the way. It is not always convenient to reach out to an attorney or comb through the mounds of information online, and this book will help you get the answers you need when you need them.

The book is organized into three main sections. Section one is all about representation options including how to keep your costs down, resources for representing yourself, and whether you even need an attorney.

Section two contains procedural steps and insider information about filing for divorce, how to identify and organize your materials, and how to present your case in court. This section will give you practical tips like how you can make a child support payment to the Support Payment Clearinghouse and how many copies of documents you need. It's useful information that only comes from experience- they don't teach this stuff in law school.

Section three is the substantive information (the law of divorce, custody, property, etc.). If you have a question about how to divide property, this section is where you will find your answers.

Use this book as a reference. You can jump around, flip through it, or read it cover to cover. We have also added lined paper and sections for you to take notes.

You will also have assignments and handouts, and this book provides a place for you to document your notes, thoughts, feelings, inventories, assets, debts, etc. This is an organizational tool you can use to represent yourself in the very best possible way while being informed about the process and the law every step of the way.

*** Disclaimer****

This book is not a substitute for legal advice and reading the book does not create an attorney client relationship or any of the benefits and privileges that comes from working with an attorney. The book is provided for informational purposes only and does not constitute legal advice.

How To Prepare For Divorce

6 FAST FACTS FROM MYMODERNLAW.COM

STEP 1: ASSESS YOUR GOALS AND GATHER YOUR RESOURCES

Gather your resources: you will need money, credit, and support to get through this process. Determine what you have available so that you can use these resources wisely and not run out of money midway through a divorce or be unable to afford a deposit on the new place you want. Make a realistic three year plan to guide you through the transition.

STEP 2: PLAN YOUR FINANCES

Get an accurate idea of all your resources and document of all of the household income. That means gathering all your pay stubs, tax returns, bank statements, and retirement accounts. Next - create a budget. Look at the cost of child care, transportation and moving. If you will need to secure health insurance, get with a broker to determine how much you can plan to spend. You will need this information in order to make a plan and for the affidavit of financial information, arguably one of the most important documents in your divorce.

STEP 3: PREPARE AND PLAN FOR CUSTODY

Help the children cope and plan for parenting time. You and your spouse should have a serious talk about how and when to tell the kids. If both of you can support them in this, it will be the single most important thing you can do to help your children transition. Never bad mouth your children's mother or father. Remember that child support will change based on parenting time arrangements, so that means there is a financial element to the discussion.

STEP 4: ASSESS YOUR PERSONAL BALANCE SHEET

Make a list of assets and debts to create a personal balance sheet. Having this updated balance sheet will help the planning process and financial decisions you make related to property division. Include all of your assets, marital and non-marital, and the date it was acquired, the value at the time of marriage, the value at the end of marriage and whether any marital monies went into the asset.

STEP 5: FOLLOW SOCIAL RULES & TAKE STEPS TO PROTECT YOURSELF

Social media is great, but now's the time to get off-line and go dark on social media. If you must post online, remember that anything you post can be used against you. Also, block your ex as a friend, and make sure any 'friends' can't make you look bad. Don't forget to change the passwords on all your accounts!

STEP 6: ASSEMBLE YOUR SUPPORT TEAM

The first advisor to consult is a divorce lawyer, preferably one who limits his or her entire practice to divorce law. An attorney can assist in creating a strategy and help add other advisors to the team. This may be a good time to connect with a mental health provider, and a Life Transition Coach to help with emotional issues. In some instances, it may also be appropriate to hire a private investigator or an accountant.

MODERN LAW

ATTEND OUR NEXT WEBINAR
MYMODERNLAW.COM/WEBINAR

PART 1

Chapter 1
Everything You Need to Know about Attorneys

First: Do you even need an attorney?

Finding the right attorney for you right from the start can save you thousands of dollars and hours of heartache – and give you a better outcome. This chapter will walk you through how to choose a divorce lawyer and provide step-by-step instructions for making the best choice for you and your needs.

The benefits of using an attorney

Using a lawyer can make a huge difference in reducing the stress you feel during the separation process and divorce. A lawyer who truly listens to you and responds appropriately can greatly reduce your fear, uncertainty and confusion. A good attorney will help your case move along smoothly, with fewer unwelcome surprises and bumps in the road.

Sometimes you need an attorney to help navigate the muddy waters of divorce. Some issues and matters require an attorney to turn a case around, handle a difficult opposing party, or simply protect your rights.

Arizona Community Property Laws can be very complicated when you have large or co-mingled marital estates. A lawyer can help you decide which of your belongings are community (marital) property and which are separate property, and advise you how the court will divide that property. A lawyer will also be able to assist you in drafting a separation agreement or Rule 69 agreement in order to document arrangements with your spouse and lock in any agreements you have reached.

There may be tricky issues that apply to you and your divorce. For example, strategies for claiming Social Security could be very important. If you have been married for at least 10 years, you qualify for Social Security spousal benefits. Similarly, if you want to pay off debt, you may be able to use your divorce as a way to avoid penalties for early retirement withdrawals.

A lawyer can also advise you if an unexpected problem comes up. For instance, if your spouse files for bankruptcy before you receive money due to you in a property settlement. Likewise, a lawyer may be able to help you creatively get rid of debt by using the bankruptcy of one spouse to wipe out the community debt of both spouses.

An attorney can help facilitate proper service of court paperwork on your spouse. A lawyer can advise you on how much money, if any, you should pay or receive for child support, or whether you may be entitled to or owe spousal maintenance.

To find the best divorce attorney for you, I recommend that you meet with, or consult with, several attorneys. This will be time – and money – well spent.

How to prepare for your initial consultation with an attorney

At Modern Law, we charge $250 for our initial consultation. Understandably, our potential clients would like to know how to make the most out of that time and get the best value for their money. They want to feel confident they will walk away from the consultation with information, answers to their questions, and a clear strategy for moving forward.

Perhaps even more important is that the firm be a good fit for your needs. Notice here I said "firm" and not just the attorney. The firm is the team that will be working on your case. This includes your team of attorneys, paralegals, law clerks, and billing department. You want to make sure you are comfortable with the whole team by the time you are done with your initial consultation.

Questions to ask in your first consultation

Here are some questions you can consider asking during your initial consultation. If you meet with more than one attorney, consider asking the same questions of each attorney so that you can compare their responses when making your decision.

- Who will work on my case?

- What is the educational training and experience of the lawyers who will be working on my case?
- How many cases like mine has your firm handled in the past year?
- What are your average fees in cases like mine?
- What do you think my case is going to cost?
- How often will I receive a bill to let me know what my fee status is and what is going on in my case?
- What does the fee include?
- What are your policies with regard to payment of fees, returning phone calls, providing copies of all correspondence and other documents, and keeping me informed about the progress of my case?
- How long will I wait to get an appointment when I need to come in again?
- What hours are you available on the telephone and in the office?
- Are my goals realistic?
- What problems can you foresee?
- How will we solve those problems?
- How will you accomplish my goals?
- How long will it all take?
- How often do you go to court?
- Do you prefer litigating a case to settling the case? If so, why?

Additionally, the lawyer will want to know some preliminary information from you, including:

- Is there an existing case number?
- Are there any pending hearings scheduled with the court?
- If you have a decree or order already in place, please bring a copy with you.
- Is the opposing party represented? If so, by whom, and how have they treated you so far?
- Is this a IV-D case (meaning the state has an interest in the child support case)?
- What are your questions? We suggest you write down any questions you have in advance. That way, we can make sure to get to all of your questions and address all of your concerns.

What else does your attorney need to know?

What are the current issues you are facing? Who are the players? For instance, is the new wife a major problem for your children? How old are the children and how do they feel about the situation? We really want to understand the dynamics and background of what has been going on with your family. Tell us your story. We want to understand what keeps you up at night and what your primary objectives are. What is the ideal outcome? How do you picture yourself a year from now? Where do you live? Where do you work? What is the schedule you have with your children?

Payment Considerations

Do you have special payment terms or parameters you are looking for? Let the attorney you consult with know what you have in mind. By having an idea in advance of your budget or budget parameters, we can design a solution that best fits your needs. For instance, if your grandmother is giving you the money for your divorce, but she will give it to you over a three-month period of time, let us know. Do you have deadlines that must be met that have not already been addressed?

Other questions that may be relevant

- Is there any history of abuse or addiction between the parties or children?
- Do the children have any special needs?
- Are there any concerns about extended family members or significant others?
- What are the retirement assets?
- Do you own property together including houses or land? If so, when was it pur- chased and with what funds?
- Did either of you bring money or property into the marriage?
- Did anyone inherit money during the marriage?
- Has anyone spent money behind the other's back on things like gambling, affairs, or prostitutes?
- Is there anything significant going on in your sex life? (I know this seems personal, but in one recent case, we found out the marriage had never been consummated due to impotence. We were able to secure an annulment instead of divorce for our client.)
- Is there a history of mental illness with either party?
- Does one party control all of the finances or any other aspect of the relationship?

- Are there religious differences or disagreements between the parties?
- Is one party dependent on financial support from the other?
- How long have you been married or separated?
- Does either party want to move?
- Has everyone in the family lived in Arizona for the last 90 days? Have the children lived in Arizona for at least six months?
- Do you own any property out of state?
- Do either of you own any interests in any businesses?
- Do you know of all of the accounts and financial institutions? Will you have access to the usernames and passwords? Will you be able to print the statements?
- Does anyone have any life insurance policies, stocks, or bonds?
- Has anyone been charged with any crimes?
- Is there a pre-nuptial or post-nuptial agreement?
- Is there student loan debt and was it used for living expenses?
- Are there any pending lawsuits? Has anyone suffered an injury in the last two years that could give rise to a lawsuit?

This is by no means an exhaustive list of potential issues, but it should give you an idea of issues that may be relevant to your case. While an initial consultation won't be able to cover your entire life story, you'll want an attorney who will strive to make it as informative, helpful and productive as possible.

Based on the answers you receive to your questions, your observations about the lawyer's style, and how you feel after the interview is over, you should be able to tell if the lawyer you've met with is the right lawyer for you.

Although initial interviews can be very intense, you should also experience some relief if you've met with a lawyer who will be good for you. If you notice that you are not feeling better after the meeting, take it as a sign that you should continue your search. When you find a lawyer with the right mix of energy, dedication, wisdom and insight, you will recognize that they are the lawyer for you.

How do you know if you have hired a bad attorney?

Many times, people change attorneys mid-stream or in the course of their case. They wonder whether this can be a "bad sign" for the judge. The fact is, if you have gone through three attorneys before your temporary orders hearing, then yes, this is a sign that you may be a difficult client. However, it is not a red flag or unusual for a client to change attorneys. How do you know if you should be changing attorneys?

You have no idea what's going on in your case

If your calls are not being returned, your emails are unanswered for days, and you never see the documents that are being filed on your behalf, you may have a communication problem.

You need to direct the objectives of your family law case. Your attorney has a duty to communicate with you about what's being filed, what is going on, and what the opposing party is communicating to your attorney.

We need to know what's going on with you and your children and your ex. We need to know if your objectives change and that you agree with everything we are saying within our pleadings on your behalf.

You are not receiving regular bills or have no idea where your money has gone.

Fee disputes are the number-one reason attorneys and clients break up. We believe that transparency and predictability are essential for a healthy attorney/ client relationship. For our traditional advanced fee clients, we invoice clients two times every month in order to make sure clients are informed about everything going on in their case. We also utilize a hybrid fee agreement of flat fees and hourly billing in order to increase predictability and uniformity for clients. Additionally, clients have the option of choosing a flat fee that covers all attorney costs no matter how long the case takes. The actual flat fee will be determined based on your individual case and will be worked out with you and your attorney.

Remember, using an attorney can make a difference, not only in how you feel but also in how you fare. Your inexperience with or false assumptions about the law can hurt you. If you never talk to an attorney about your spouse's settlement proposal or if you never have settlement papers reviewed by someone who can advocate for your interests, you could get the short end of the bargain without even knowing it. The lawyer you choose, of course, has to be smart enough about the law to tell you the things you should know.

Even if you still trust your spouse, this is not a time to be foolhardy. You may be entitled to things you don't even know about. Just as bad, your spouse may be consulting with an attorney without your knowing about it, so the playing field may not be as even as you believe.

For instance, I recently met with a client whose wife had purchased their marital home in her name only 15 years ago. He mistakenly believed that she was entitled to the more than $100,000 in equity in the home as her separate property. During our initial consultation, he learned he was entitled to half of the equity! A small $250 investment became a $50,000 gain for the client!

In other words, don't assume your spouse has good intentions just because your spouse tells you that his or her offer to you is fair and equitable. You can listen, as much or as little as you care to, to what your spouse has to say, but judge your spouse's offer for yourself, based on all the information you need in order to evaluate that offer. Even if you represent yourself, we strongly recommend you have *at least one meeting* with an attorney to check out your understandings with an objective, trained person.

Why you shouldn't procrastinate

A lot of people put off going to see a lawyer. But delaying a visit with a lawyer is a major mistake.

One of the most common reasons for not going to see an attorney is denial:

- "My marriage isn't really all that bad, things are going to get better."
- "Lawyers are scary, and I'd feel too intimidated."
- "I can't talk to a stranger about all the distress I'm having or I'll fall apart."

Denial also may be linked to financial worries:

- "I can't afford the fees lawyers charge."

- "Even though I have the money and know I need a lawyer, the lawyer is going to bleed me dry and I don't know how to keep that from happening."

These are common feelings and situations, and each is surmountable. If you decide you need a lawyer, you should be able to overcome these barriers and find solid legal representation.

Another reason that people don't go to speak with attorneys is they don't know when and why lawyers should be consulted.

- "I don't need a lawyer right now."
- "I can do anything better than anyone else"
- "There's nothing a lawyer could do for me that I can't do for myself."

These reasons for delay stems basically from a lack of familiarity with what lawyers do. Occasionally it stems from personal overconfidence, but that's a dangerous attitude if you've haven't taken the time to thoroughly educate yourself and consult with someone who has more experience.

Most people do realize, however, that lawyers have specialized knowledge and skills. Unfortunately, these same people may not recognize that separation and divorce law is full of highly technical rules and traps for the unwary. The law is like poker, and maybe just as risky: If you don't know all the rules and how to play to win, you can lose the game.

The fact is, you don't just need a lawyer when you've been sued or have to go to court. Legal advice in advance can prevent certain problems from ever arising, and properly timed legal advice can potentially reduce the dimensions of existing problems. This kind of preventative use of a lawyer can save you heartache, time, and money. If you decide you need a lawyer, go and see an attorney as soon as possible, rather than putting off the appointment.

Gathering information about your prospective attorney

Gathering the information you need is not as difficult as you might think. One easy way to gather information about attorneys is to ask people you trust and respect for leads, including not only the names of lawyers but also referrals to other people who might be able to suggest names. Friends, relatives, neighbors, casual acquaintances and work associates are possible sources of leads, as well as people you do business with.

In particular, mental health professionals and clergy who engage in crisis couples' counseling and general marriage counseling will probably have considerable information to share with you about the local domestic relations bar. You should also try to find out some of the names of a lawyer's satisfied clients. However, keep in mind you probably won't be able to obtain this information from the attorney directly, because a client or former client's name remains confidential unless the client consents to the disclosure.

If you can, talk to clients or former clients about their personal experiences with the lawyer. People in your area who have actually been through separation and divorce can be your most valuable resources in selecting an attorney, as they will have formed opinions about their own lawyers and opposing counsel (your ex's attorney). You might also talk to other lawyers you know about a particular family law attorney's reputation.

The online review website Avvo.com reviews all lawyers for areas of law. You can check out an attorney's reviews from clients, endorsements from other attorneys, and even their disciplinary track record.

Another source of information is the courthouse personnel who regularly interact with local attorneys. These first-hand observers of attorneys-in-action may be far more valuable to your decision-making process than lawyer advertisements or the listings in the Martindale-Hubbell Law Directory.

Still, advertisements and directory entries can provide additional information about the kinds of cases a lawyer handles, where he or she went to school, and the colleagues with whom the lawyer practices. You might also ask, when you start visiting lawyer's offices, if the firm has a brochure that you can have. The specialized training and knowledge of a lawyer you are considering is also something to inquire about. A lawyer who stays current with changes in the law of property division, custody/ legal decision-making and parenting time, child support and spousal maintenance will probably give you better advice than one who doesn't.

Similarly, a specialized lawyer's advice can be more custom-tailored to your needs and goals because a specialist's depth will provide him or her with more creative and flexible solutions to new problems. Just like when you decide between a general medical practitioner and a specialist to deal with a health issue, you need to diagnose the complexity of the concerns in your case before settling on the lawyer who could most properly advise you. Make sure to ask the attorney how many hours of continuing legal education they attend each year. Consider asking if the attorney provides instruction on continuing legal education, and what other training they have received.

Before you make a final decision …

Most vital, of course, is that you meet any attorney who has been recommended to you before you decide if the lawyer is right for you. Your first contact with the lawyer may be by telephone. Sometimes the phone conversation alone tells you enough about the person to let you know whether you want to move on to the next step and actually schedule an office appointment.

If you do decide to attend an initial meeting, plan to conduct your own interview of the lawyer to learn whether you feel your needs will be understood and adequately addressed by this particular lawyer.

This point cannot be made strongly enough. No matter how strongly a particular lawyer has been recommended to you, selecting an attorney is a highly personal matter. No one else should make this decision for you. This is, after all, the person you are possibly going to retain to safeguard your rights during a time of great emotional upheaval for you, to structure a settlement that is as favorable as possible to you, and to advise you on such highly technical matters as the potential tax consequences of a proposed settlement. Your sense of who the lawyer is as a person will be extremely important in predicting how much and what kind of attention the lawyer will give to your case.

The first meeting

Here are some signals you should watch for in the first meeting. Keep looking if:

- If the lawyer you meet with does not strike you as a person in whom you can be confident, as a person who will act in your best interests, or as a person who can reach a resolution of your case efficiently and sensitively.
- If your meeting did not result in a feeling of personal rapport or if you felt the lawyer was not very attentive to your questions and concerns, look elsewhere.
- If he or she appears to be disorganized, or if you can't follow most of what the lawyer is telling you, or if you suspect the lawyer doesn't know the field very well.

Trust your first impression

First impressions are often lasting impressions. If you are uncomfortable with a lawyer's practice philosophy or style during an initial meeting, it is not likely you will grow to like the attorney a great deal more as time goes on. In one sense, picking a lawyer is a matter of personal taste. You are probably not going to feel very good anyway as you go through separation and divorce, given the huge emotional and financial issues you may be dealing with. There is absolutely no reason, then, to make yourself feel even worse by selecting a lawyer you just plain don't like.

Policies and fees

Pay attention as well to your responses to the information you pick up during an office interview regarding the lawyer's policies, including attorney fees. At the out- set you should be given a clear explanation of the attorney's billing and collection policies.

- Will you be billed at an hourly rate? If so, what is that rate; does it vary among personnel in the law firm; are there different hourly rates for office and court-room work?
- How will you be charged for other expenses such as photocopying, secretarial time, postage, and like items?
- Are you expected to pay in advance of receiving services?
- If there is a "retainer" (initial advance deposit), is it refundable or non-refundable if the work is terminated or completed before the entire deposit has been used?
- Is a flat fee (a fixed price for a defined legal job) available from this law practice?
- Will your billing statements be sufficiently detailed for you to determine exactly what work has been performed?

- Will there be a written fee agreement between you and your attorney?

Especially in family law, where the issues are so emotionally charged and clients are understandably under very great stress, the issue of fees can poison the relationship between client and lawyer if misunderstandings aren't cleared up early on.

You are entitled to know how you will be charged for the work done for you, what other fees might be assessed to your case, and how you are expected to pay your bill. Don't settle for vague answers to questions about fees. No lawyer is likely to know exactly how much it will cost to handle your case; but every lawyer should be willing to tell you as much as he or she can about fees.

If the fee quoted to you is so low that it is almost too good to be true, that may be a very bad sign. Low fees usually mean one of two things: either the attorney is hungry for business (which may mean the lawyer is inexperienced or that other people have found out this lawyer is not very good), or he or she doesn't really expect to finish your case for the quoted fee (which means the retainer amount is no indication of how much you will eventually spend). Do some sleuthing to determine if the attorney is a novice or if the quoted fee is unrealistic in light of the work that will need to be done.

If the quoted fee is unrealistic, that can also be a sure sign that the lawyer has lots of clients signing up at those bargain-basement prices. All those clients are poorly served because the lawyer has too little time to spend on each individual's case. Waits (for appointments, for returned phone calls, for work to be drafted, for court dates) will be long in such offices; and you may wind up feeling like you have just gotten lost in the crowd.

You may also wind up paying the "cheaper" lawyer more money in the long run, based on such a lawyer's lack of specialized knowledge and inefficiencies in the lawyer's office. In sum, large caseloads do not translate into quality legal services. Stay away from the lawyer who appears to offer large discounts.

Notes

_____

_____

_____

_____

_____

_____

_____

_____

_____

_____

_____

_____

_____

_____

Chapter 2

Divorce Fees: You Have Options

When it comes to paying for a divorce, you have many options for what will work best for you and your budget.

Whether you are representing yourself with the assistance of an attorney or you are using an attorney in a traditional sense, this section will give you the information you need. This includes what a divorce typically costs, how to save money in your divorce, your outside-the-box options to pay for divorce, flat fee divorce options, online divorce, and do-it-yourself divorce.

How much does it cost to get divorced?

Many people want to know what a divorce typically costs. It depends. The average cost, nationwide, is roughly $20,000—for EACH spouse. However, I know of people who spend less than $500 to get divorced and others who spend more than $100,000!

The biggest factor in how much a divorce costs, and how much you will spend to get divorced, is whether you will do it yourself, use a paralegal/document preparer, or have an attorney or lawyer represent you in your divorce. We will discuss each option below. Regardless of which representation option you choose, there are always things you can do to save money in your divorce. Proper planning and preparation will help you avoid spending too much during the process.

How to Save Money in Your Divorce

Follow this step-by-step plan and rack up the savings.

CAN YOU DIVORCE WITHOUT AN ATTORNEY?

The 10 questions You MUST Ask Yourself Before You Attempt a Do-It-Yourself Divorce

ACCESSLEGALDOCS.COM • MYMODERNLAW.COM

1. ARE YOU ON TIME FOR MEETINGS AND DEADLINES?

It is essential that you file documents on time and show up for court early. Missing these deadlines can have disastrous consequences for your case.

2. DO YOU HAVE THE TIME?

Ask yourself if you really have the time to make it happen? Will you be able to make it to the courthouse during the day (during business hours)? If you are representing yourself you will need to be at the courthouse during business hours to file documents and appear at hearings. Using a lawyer means you would need to be at the courthouse less.

3. DO YOU PREPARE AND FILE YOUR OWN INCOME TAX RETURNS?

If you are comfortable filing your own taxes, this may be a good indication you will be equipped to file your own court documents. Court forms can be complicated, much like income tax returns. You will be expected to read lengthy instructions and pay close attention to detail when completing your documents.

4. ARE YOU COMFORTABLE DOING ONLINE RESEARCH?

Information is available to you on all of the rules and statutes. Most people find it overwhelming, but some love the research. If you like learning and researching, you will be well-suited for a DIY divorce. Most people do not know the law and rules that control their cases.

Learning the law and rules for your case is required to be successful. While the court may provide forms for you to fill out and file, you will likely have questions. Court staff can only give you limited answers to your questions because of their duty to be fair to all parties.

Pro Per (self-represented) litigants are held to the SAME STANDARD as attorneys. If you do not take the time to learn the law and rules of your case, you are unlikely to be successful. You may also feel frustrated and unfairly treated because you do not understand what is happening.

5. CAN YOU COMMUNICATE ON PAPER AND IN COURT?

Are you likely to be clear and calm when you stand up and speak in court and in documents? Do you communicate well both orally and in writing? Do you feel comfortable articulating your position as it relates to the law? Representing yourself means you must attend all the scheduled appearances with the judge or commissioner. At these appearances, you will be required to speak clearly and logically while presenting your case.

It is even more important that you draft your documents clearly and convincingly. The judge will read prehearing statements before trial. Sometimes a judge has already made up their mind prior to anyone speaking in court. If the other party has a lawyer and you do not, you cannot count on the other lawyer to help you or speak for you. You must speak to the court yourself.

6. DO YOU EASILY GET ANGRY UNDER STRESS? HOW WELL DO YOU DEAL WITH YOUR EMOTIONS?

On a scale of 1-10, if your emotions are above a 6, you will likely need representation. Coming to court can be difficult and stressful for anyone, even with a lawyer. Family law is personal; there is no way around it. Honestly assess whether it will be difficult to control your emotions in the courtroom and while speaking. You may also find that your good judgment is clouded by your stress or anger.

You must be courteous at all times to court staff, the judge or commissioner, and the other party to your case. You cannot interrupt the other party, or the judge or commissioner, while they are speaking.

7. ARE YOU OFTEN FRUSTRATED BY RULES YOU THINK ARE UNFAIR OR SHOULD NOT APPLY TO YOU?

All types of cases are controlled by rules and procedures. These rules and procedures are in place to give everyone a level playing field. Though a rule may seem silly or wrong, the rule must be followed to make sure your case is fair.

8. CAN YOU MAKE DECISIONS AND STICK TO THEM?

Most court processes are formal and lasting. Once you make a claim, a statement, or a filing, it is difficult to make changes. Any doubts or questions should be considered and answered before you start.

9. CAN YOU LIVE WITH SOME MISTAKES?

If you represent yourself, you are likely to make some mistakes. If you regret decisions, or often dwell on actions you have taken, you may cause yourself stress and anxiety. You may also hurt your ability to be successful in your case.

10. WHAT IS AT STAKE IN YOUR CASE? DO YOU AND THE OTHER PARTY GET ALONG?

Every case is important, but some cases may have a bigger effect on you because of the large amount of money (or property) involved, or other people involved (like children). Cases with more money or people to consider are more complicated. Using a lawyer will make these cases less confusing and upsetting, and prevent mistakes that could be difficult or impossible to correct after the case is over.

If you and the other party had a relationship that included physical or emotional abuse, you may have trouble keeping a steady emotional state. Being calm and logical is necessary to make good decisions in your case. Using a lawyer may help you keep a safe and comfortable distance from the other party.

If you feel the other party is good at "hiding" money or property (like on tax forms), or if you have no idea about the other party's financial status, using a lawyer may be helpful in locating the other party's finances and collecting on a judgment or settlement.

Many people represent themselves because they have no other option. Others determine that the cost of an attorney is not worth the benefit of full-scope representation. The quiz above can help you determine whether you are a good candidate for a do-it-yourself divorce.

Think about the issues that must be resolved in your case, including custody issues, property issues, debts, alimony, and any other issues that will need to be worked out. Consider the range of outcomes you can live with for each issue below and think about your best case, worst case, and the happy medium you can live with.

Common issues in a divorce include:

- Property and debt division
- Family businesses
- Student loans
- Mortgages
- Credit card debt
- Separate or premarital assets or debts
- Inheritances
- Insurance settlements
- Property
- Legal decision making
- Domestic violence
- Addiction issues
- Mental health issues
- Differences in religion
- Differences in schooling preferences
- Differences in medical treatment opinions
- Parenting time
- Consider work schedules
- Consider how far apart you live
- Consider where the children go to school
- How old are the children?
- What are their preferences?
- Child support
- You need to know all income
- Child care costs
- Non-joint children

- Medical costs
- Spousal maintenance paid and received
- Parenting time schedule
- Spousal maintenance/alimony
- Does one party rely on the other?
- What will your budget be?
- Where will you live?

Gather your resources

Once you have a practical idea of the issues you will be addressing, you can begin gathering your resources. Gathering your resources refers to both financial and emotional resources.

Consider how much you are willing to spend to achieve your objectives. Do a cost-benefit analysis associated with your best case and worst case scenarios regarding the issues we have outlined above. For instance, if you have hundreds of thousands of dollars at stake, you should be prepared to defend your position and make what- ever short-term arrangements you need to in order to protect your future.

If you or your spouse have no children and are dividing debt, then you will probably not need an attorney to fight over the division of debt. If you do end up using an attorney, their costs should be kept to a minimum in order to ensure you do not spend more on fees than you would gain from the financial benefits of legal representation.

Also, gather your emotional support resources. One of the reasons people end up spending so much money is that they tend to use their lawyer as a friend or sounding board. While a certain amount of emotional support should be expected from your attorney, you should not go to your attorney for advice and support on non-legal issues. They are not equipped to give you good counseling and they are far too expensive to use in that role.

Know your options

Depending on your budget and the issues in your case, you will need to determine whether you want to take care of your divorce without the assistance of an attorney—

in other words, to determine whether you are a good candidate for a do-it- yourself divorce.

Options to Pay for Your Divorce

Determining the cost of your divorce and how to pay for it can be broken down into two categories.

1. What are your representation options?
2. What are your funding options?

First, let's look at your representation options. These will include the following approaches that we detail in the following pages:

- Do-it-yourself divorce Using a CDLP or paralegal
- Online divorce
- Traditional attorney representation
- Alternative arrangements with attorneys
- Flat fee divorce
- Limited scope divorce

Do-It-Yourself Divorce

Should you DIY? Between 80% and 90% of individuals represent themselves in family court. Sometimes this works out very well. Other times, it can be disastrous. If you decide to represent yourself, there are things you can do to avoid disaster.

To determine whether you are a good candidate for a do-it-yourself divorce, you should analyze how complex the legal issues are and then consider your personality traits and disposition.

First, how legally complicated is your case?

How many of the issues above did you identify as relevant to your case? How long have you been married? How many of the issues below are in dispute? Do you understand the law and procedures?

In general, if you have more than five of the issues below, or have any substantial assets, you may **not** be a good candidate for a do-it-yourself divorce.

Check the possible issues in your divorce:

Property and debt division
- Family businesses
- Student loans
- Mortgages
- Credit card debt
- Separate or premarital assets or debts
- Inheritances
- Insurance settlements

Legal decision making
- Domestic violence issues
- Addiction issues
- Mental health issues
- Differences in religion
- Differences in schooling preferences
- Differences in medical treatment opinions

Parenting Time
- Consider work schedules
- Consider how far apart you live
- Consider where the children go to school
- How old are the children?
- What are their preferences?

Child Support
- You need to know all income sources
- Child care costs
- Non-joint children
- Medical costs
- Spousal maintenance paid and received

- Parenting time schedule

Spousal maintenance/alimony
- Does one party rely on the other?
- What will your budget be?
- Where will you live?

Are you emotionally and practically suited for the do-it-yourself divorce?

The next step in the analysis of whether or not you are a good candidate for the do-it-yourself divorce is more practical. You will need to determine how emotionally complicated things are for you right now, and whether your personality traits lend themselves to successful do-it-yourself representation.

Here are some practical questions to ask:

1. <u>Are you on time for meetings and deadlines?</u> It is essential that you file documents on time and show up for court early. Missing these deadlines can have disastrous consequences for your case.

2. <u>Do you have the time to make it happen?</u> Can you make it to the courthouse during the day (during business hours)? If you are representing yourself, you will need to be at the courthouse during business hours to file documents and appear at hearings. Using a lawyer means you would need to be at the courthouse less.

3. <u>Do you fill out and file your own income tax returns</u>? If you are comfortable filing your own taxes, this may be a good indication you will be equipped to file your own court documents. Court forms can be complicated, much like income tax returns. You will be expected to read lengthy instructions and pay close attention to detail when completing your documents.

4. <u>Are you comfortable doing research, either in a library or on a computer?</u> Information is available to you on all of the rules and statutes. Most people find it overwhelming, but some love the research. If you like learning and researching, you will be well-suited for a DIY divorce. Most people do not know the law and rules that control their cases.

    Learning the law and rules for your case is required to be successful. While the court may provide forms for you to fill out and file, you will likely have questions.

Court staff can only give you limited answers to your questions because of their duty to be fair to all parties.

Pro Per (self-represented) litigants are held to the SAME STANDARD as attorneys. If you do not take the time to learn the law and rules of your case, you are unlikely to be successful. You may also feel frustrated and unfairly treated because you do not understand what is happening.

5. <u>Are you likely to be clear and calm when you stand up and speak in court and in documents?</u> Do you communicate well both orally and in writing? Do you feel comfortable articulating your position as it relates to the law?

   Representing yourself means you must attend all the scheduled appearances with the judge or commissioner. At these appearances, you will be required to speak clearly and logically while presenting your case.

   It is even more important that you draft your documents clearly and convincingly. The judge will read prehearing statements before trial. Sometimes a judge has already made up their mind prior to anyone speaking in court.

   If the other party has a lawyer and you do not, you cannot count on the other lawyer to help you or speak for you. You must speak to the court yourself.

6. <u>Do you easily get angry under stress?</u> Where are you at emotionally? On a scale of 1-10, if your emotions are above a 6, you will likely need representation.
   Coming to court can be difficult and stressful for anyone, even with a lawyer. Family law is personal; there is no way around it. Honestly assess whether it will be difficult to control your emotions in the courtroom and while speaking. You may also find that your good judgment is clouded by your stress or anger.

   You must be courteous at all times to court staff, the judge or commissioner, and the other party to your case. You cannot interrupt the other party, or the judge or commissioner, while they are speaking.

7. <u>Are you often frustrated by rules you think are unfair or should not apply to you?</u> All types of cases are controlled by rules and procedures. These rules and procedures are in place to give everyone a level playing field. Though a rule may seem silly or wrong, the rule must be followed to make sure your case is fair.

8. <u>Can you make decisions and stick to them?</u> Most court processes are formal and lasting. Once you make a claim, a statement, or a filing, it is difficult to make

changes. Any doubts or questions should be considered and answered before you start.

9. <u>Can you live with some mistakes?</u> If you represent yourself, you are likely to make some mistakes. If you regret decisions, or often dwell on actions you have taken, you may cause yourself stress and anxiety. You may also hurt your ability to be successful in your case.

10. <u>What is at stake in your case?</u> Do you and the other party get along?

Every case is important, but some cases may have a bigger effect on you because of the large amount of money (or property) involved, or other people involved (like children). Cases with more money or people to consider are more complicated.

Using a lawyer will make these cases less confusing and upsetting, and prevent mistakes that could be difficult or impossible to correct after the case is over.

If you and the other party had a relationship that included physical or emotional abuse, you may have trouble keeping a steady emotional state. Being calm and logical is necessary to make good decisions in your case. Using a lawyer may help you keep a safe and comfortable distance from the other party.

If you feel the other party is good at "hiding" money or property (like on tax forms), or if you have no idea about the other party's financial status, using a lawyer may be helpful in locating the other party's finances and collecting on a judgment or settlement.

Many people represent themselves because they have no other option. Others deter- mine that the cost of an attorney is not worth the benefit of full-scope representation. The quiz above can help you determine whether you are a good candidate for a do-it-yourself divorce.

Final thoughts on the do-it-yourself divorce

While Arizona allows self-representation in divorce cases, it holds the party to the same standard as lawyers. If you miss a deadline, or sign a divorce agreement without fully understanding the terms, you're out of luck. You can't plead ineffective assistance of counsel—the courts presume you knew all the risks beforehand, and you'll have to take the consequences.

There are no do-overs. I have spoken to many litigants who represented themselves and have come to me for help after their case has gone horribly wrong. Unfortunately, the vast majority of the time I cannot set aside the ruling. Property division is non-modifiable. Spousal maintenance is a one-time shot. You cannot go back after you have waived alimony and get spousal maintenance.

Do not try to represent yourself if the divorce is contested. Get help, even if it's behind the scenes. It will be worth the small investment to get some help on the major issues.

DIY divorce — tips and tools

Take advantage of free resources. Before you file anything, educate yourself about your local laws and procedures. Check out any local free resources geared toward education, including seminars, webinars, articles, and/or consultations with attorneys. You'll find many helpful free tools on our website at www.mymodernlaw.com.

If you are not a good candidate for a DIY divorce, but your budget will not allow for a traditional attorney, you have several options, including certified legal document preparers, paralegals and limited-scope attorneys.

2. What is a certified legal document preparer (CLDP)?

Did you know that if someone is not a lawyer or a CLDP, completing legal forms for you to file is the unauthorized practice of law? It is prohibited. This is because legal documents have lasting and serious consequences. Only those who are trained to understand the consequences and ramifications are allowed to prepare legal documents.

A certified legal document preparer (CLDP) is someone who is certified by the state to help prepare legal documents for people who do not have lawyers. This is an excellent option for people who have a limited budget, no lawyer, and they want support while they represent themselves.

Some of the requirements to become a CLDP include passing a background and fingerprint check, passing a rigorous examination, and having at least two years of law-related experience (usually by working at a law firm or a court) and/or at least 24 credits of law-related education.

Because of this last requirement, many CLDPs are also paralegals.

Access Legal is a service company that grew out of Modern Law to help self-representing individuals in Arizona! With Access Legal you can find local documents and resources for low cost and even NO cost. Be wary of companies simply providing "forms" to all states. They are not likely to offer all of the resources you need in order to protect yourself.

What's the difference between a CLDP and a paralegal?

Unlike a paralegal, a CLDP does not work under the supervision of a lawyer. A CLDP must make it clear to any customer that the CLDP is not a lawyer and cannot give legal advice. They do not have a lawyer checking their work or giving them guidance or providing supervision.

What can a CLDP tell me?

A CLDP can give a customer general factual information pertaining to legal rights, procedures, or options available.

For example, a CLDP cannot answer the question, "Should I ask for spousal maintenance?" But he or she can show the client the statute regarding what the court considers when deciding whether to grant spousal maintenance (in this case, ARS 25-319).

In short, a CLDP can give you legal information, but not advice.

Why would I use a CLDP?

In a family court matter like a divorce, unless the relationship is particularly contentious and/or the community property/debt situation is particularly complex, a person may benefit from using a CLDP, especially at the beginning stages of the case; after all, a

CLDP is less expensive than hiring a lawyer, and many of the documents required to begin a divorce proceeding may seem complicated and intimidating. In short, you may save money but still be confident knowing your documents have been correctly created.

Access Legal offers statewide document preparation, with documents developed by local attorneys for the local court system. We offer webinars, e-books, workbooks, referrals and more. Our CLDP has more than 10 years of experience in local family law, working both under the supervision of an attorney as a paralegal and independently as a CLDP. Many clients seamlessly move from working with attorneys to CLDPs and back to the firm as necessary, or they DIY with the assistance of a qualified and competent CLDP.

Traditional Arrangements with Attorneys

Traditional attorney arrangements include depositing an advanced fee or "retainer" into a trust account for the attorney to bill against at his/her hourly rate. When the trust reaches a certain amount, the client is expected to put more money into the account.

How traditional attorney billing works

How this works in practice is that everyone who touches your case is assigned a different rate. Typically, an attorney charges between $250-$450 per hour, paralegals bill between $90-$180 per hour, and administrative staff bill between $60-$100 per hour. Then each person who touches your case tracks every minute they spend talking to you, reading your emails, opening mail related to your case, drafting, researching, setting up your file, etc. You then receive periodic invoices telling you exactly what your attorney and the firm have done on your case. There is no cap and there is no guarantee of results.

The dangers of the arrangement

I have learned so much from working with lawyers from the client's perspective. I recently received a very unpleasant surprise, and it wasn't the first time it has happened. I hired an attorney for a project. We came up with an estimated retainer. I deposited the money and off they went. Months later, after the project was completed, I got an invoice. Undoubtedly the invoice well exceeded our retainer and I was annoyed, angry and feel I was wrongfully overcharged. For instance, I saw on the invoice that my

$320/hour attorney charged me for the time it took to speak with her boss, who is a $450/hour attorney.

Why am I annoyed? The lack of communication is what bothers me. As a client I prefer to know in advance when I will be invoiced and which services I will be charged for, so I know what to expect. (At Modern Law, we invoice on the 5th and 20th of each month.)

As a client, I appreciate being told what is being done on my case and how much I should expect my overall bill should cost. I want to know how my attorney is spending my hard-earned money and what they are doing on my project/case. You have a right to expect the same courtesy from your attorney.

Protect yourself from unexpected attorney bills

If you are working with an attorney in a traditional arrangement, make sure the fee agreement *expressly* states when and how often they will bill you.

Additionally, ask the attorney to tell you when it is clear that they will exceed the estimated budget/retainer. We all certainly understand that a legal budget is a moving target, subject to change with what the attorney finds while researching, or what opposing counsel may do. If an attorney simply communicates early and often, we may not like the high legal fees, but at least we will expect them.

While arrangements differ from office to office, here is how we handle the traditional arrangement at Modern Law: The client should have the ability to do a cost-benefit analysis of what we do as lawyers. For instance, the client should decide whether to file a motion to dismiss or simply respond to the untimely petition.

The client should decide whether or not we depose the opposing party. When I receive a notice of deposition for my client, he or she should be informed immediately that this will have an impact on their overall fees.

As a client, we want some skin in the game. We want to be savvy shoppers. We want input and we want to know the impact of our decisions.

Clear communication with the client also protects the lawyer. When the client decides, "YES, file the motion to dismiss," he/she will not be surprised to see it on their invoice (hopefully next week) and will be less likely to suffer billing frustrations.

Other ways to save money in your divorce

Get organized. Deliver to your attorney a complete set of the documents they have requested in an organized and easy-to-understand format. If you need assistance with this, hire someone to help you do your homework! <u>It will be much less expensive than paying an attorney to organize your documents</u>.

Be disciplined in your communications. Resist the urge to email or call your attorney every time your ex does something that you don't like. Instead, keep a journal of your thoughts and questions and put together a thorough email once a week of everything that you consider important. Alternatively, schedule a meeting to go over your questions with your attorney.

Remember your objectives. Resist the urge to get caught up in the details and drama of your case. Continue to refer to your goals and objectives and remember what you determined you "could live with." People rarely get everything they are asking for in a divorce and it makes sense to continually do a cost-benefit analysis of each and every step your attorney proposed.

By staying purposeful, you can help control your divorce costs and outcome. If you don't feel you can trust your attorney, or if you are uncomfortable in your current situation, consider making a change.

Options to Pay for Your Divorce

What are your funding options for paying for your divorce?

Many of my clients need money for representation in a divorce. Often, one spouse controls the majority of the assets, making it difficult, if not impossible, for the spouse without access to secure the representation they need in order to get an equitable distribution. Here are some options for how people typically fund their divorce.

1. **Cash or reserve funds.** For people who have the savings set aside, the easiest way to pay for an attorney is by using the savings.

2. **Credit cards.** Many people use credit cards to deposit money into a trust account or pay a flat fee for a divorce. Most attorneys accept credit cards. One possible advantage to using credit cards is that the total debt may be divided between spouses. This means if you don't have access to funds but you do have access to credit, you could end up only paying half, or even less of your attorney's fees yourself.

3. **Borrowing money from your retirement account.** Some people take money out of their retirement account in order to pay for their attorney. You may be able to avoid the penalties of cashing out a retirement fund early by using the tax code and your divorce to your advantage. Be aware, you will need to make this withdrawal before you or your spouse files for divorce. After a petition for divorce has been filed, a preliminary injunction is in place, which prohibits the withdrawal of retirement funds in most circumstances. Ask your attorney for details.

4. **Borrowing money from family or friends.** Many people receive financial assistance from their family or friends during a divorce. This may take the form of a gift or a loan. Many times this works out without any problems. But be aware that this can cause difficulties if the person who's paying wishes to control your case. At Modern Law, we make it very clear to the third parties that they are free to pay for the case, but they will not have any of the advantages that the client receives. The client alone will control the objectives of the case.

5. **Third-Party Divorce Funding.** A fifth option, and one that is rarely utilized, is third-party divorce funding. Often, clients would like the attorney to offer financing or a payment plan. This is a bad idea and probably a conflict of interest! An attorney cannot best represent a client who owes thousands of dollars to the firm. It could cloud the lawyers' judgment or affect the level of representation provided to the client. But, if the client doesn't have access to money, or family who can loan them money, what can they do?

Third-party divorce funding is becoming an increasingly viable option for clients. Two well-known companies that offer funding are:

http://www.bblchurchill.com/home.html   www.balancepointfunding.com/

A third, newer player, "Nationwide Divorce Funding," is also an option for divorcing spouses.

In my humble opinion, it is best to borrow money from financing companies, or outside sources, not from attorneys or law firms.

Next we will discuss alternative fee arrangements with divorce attorneys, which include:

- **Limited scope attorney arrangements**
- **Flat fee divorce**
- **Capped fee divorce**

Limited Scope Legal Services

Limited scope legal services mean you hire the attorney to complete tasks or phases of your case, not the whole case. They may not become your attorney of record, but you are not handing them a blank check either. You are doing parts of the case on your own, like in the do-it-yourself divorce section, but you are hiring an attorney for the pieces of the case you are not comfortable doing yourself.

MODERN LAW GAME PLAN

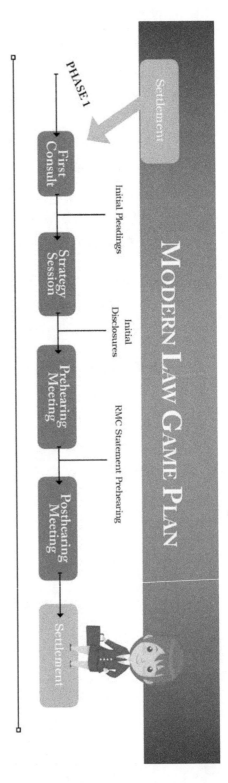

PHASE 1

Settlement

First Consult

Initial Pleadings

Strategy Session

Initial Disclosures

Prehearing Meeting

RMC Statement Prehearing

Posthearing Meeting

Settlement

PHASE 2

Case Review

Ongoing Disclosures

Prep for 3rd ACL

CAA PC

Review Report

Settlement Memo

ADR Prep

ADR

Status Conference

Settlement

PHASE 3

ID Exhibits Witnesses

Ongoing Disclosures

Finalize Positions

Prepare For Trial

Submit Exhibits

Trial

Submit Pretrial Statement

Post Hearing

Settlement

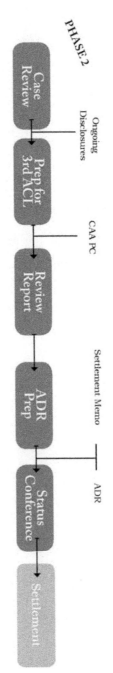

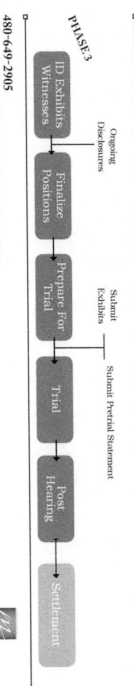

480-649-2905
1744 SOUTH VAL VISTA DRIVE, SUITE 205 MESA, AZ 85204
7272 EAST INDIAN SCHOOL ROAD, SUITE 540 SCOTTSDALE, AZ 85251

MODERN LAW

Consider using an attorney on a limited scope basis.

Just because you decide to represent yourself doesn't mean you can't use an attorney for anything. Many attorneys are now offering "limited scope" or "unbundled" legal services. This means that you hire an attorney for pieces of your case, but not to do everything. This can be a very viable option for those who have complicated issues but don't have $20,000 or more to spend on an attorney.

Consider doing the preliminary paperwork yourself, gathering documents and information, and then hiring an attorney to represent you in court. By doing some of the work yourself you can cut down on the overall costs and still get many of the benefits of having an attorney involved. You can truly craft this option to your case and budget.

Make sure you find an experienced attorney (one with at least two years experience in YOUR area) who is familiar with practicing limited scope legal services. Inexperienced attorneys will not be able to equip you with the knowledge you need if they are not responsible for your case. Likewise, if an attorney is unfamiliar with limited scope legal services, he or she may not offer the best resources or advice for working together.

I have been using limited scope legal services extensively for the last five years and have spoken both statewide and nationally on how attorneys can best use limited scope legal services. Make sure the attorney will work with you to determine the best way to use your budget and work with you on a limited scope basis.

Flat Fee Divorce Options

If you know you want an attorney to handle all aspects of your divorce, consider proposing a flat fee arrangement. This will only work if you have a good deal of cash to shell out up front, but could save you considerable money in the long term. If you are able to negotiate a flat fee with your attorney, you will not have to worry about monthly invoices or by-the-minute billing. This could make the arrangement much more beneficial and stress-free for you. However, some attorneys who work on a flat fee basis may charge between $20,000-$50,000 for a flat fee divorce.

Modern Law recently expanded our fee model to allow clients to lock in a flat fee price for their divorce or family law case. The result has been astounding. More than half of the people we talk with are signing up to take advantage of the flat fee model. In fact, we are close to being in a position of turning clients away due to the sharp increase in demand. What is going on?

1. **Flat fees bring people certainty.**
2. **Flat fees shift the risk to the attorney.**
3. **Flat fees align the objectives of the attorney and the client.**
4. **Flat fees encourage results and efficiency.**

Certainty

The flat fee divorce is very different from the traditional model. For instance, in our standard advanced fee agreement, we include language explaining that we are making no guarantees about the final *price or results* obtained through representation. You will be billed hourly (per minute actually) for every time we touch your case. The more time it takes us, the more it costs you.

The average divorce in this country costs *each side* $20,000. Your divorce may cost

$5k or it may cost $50k. There is no way of knowing or guaranteeing or capping your fees under the traditional model.

However, with the flat fee model, you know exactly what you need to budget for and how much it will cost to obtain your results. Our attorneys lock in a price with you following our initial consultation.

We have also created a calculator you can use in advance to estimate what your flat fee might be. Go to the Modern Law Flat Fee Calculator to estimate your costs.

People love the certainly of knowing that no matter how long it takes, we will get them divorced for a flat fee.

Risk shifts to the attorney

Under the traditional model, all of the risk is on the client. If the opposing party runs up your bill, there is nothing your attorney can do to prevent your bill from climbing. If the judge continues your case three times (which has happened) and you end up litigating for two years, your bill increases. If the opposing party won't disclose documents you need and we need to subpoena third parties, you will need to pay for your attorney to draft the documents, emails, and process all of the information. All of the risk is on you, the client.

Under the flat fee model, the risk now shifts to the attorney. The attorney is responsible for accomplishing a given objective for a specific price. If the attorney fails to account for all possible contingencies, they will lose money.

At Modern Law, we have always been very conscious of our clients' budget constraints. No one has an unlimited budget for legal fees, and we have always sought to be good stewards of our clients' resources. That means many times we may have forgone a deposition or discovery requests of the opposing party in order to save money for clients. With the flat fee model, we can be as creative as we would like in our legal approach without charging the client any more money! This is incredibly freeing for the attorney and makes us better advocates for our clients.

Client and attorney objectives are aligned

Your goal is to achieve favorable results for your divorce or modification or enforcement as quickly as possible. With flat fees, the attorney is also incentivized to achieve the desired outcome as quickly as possible. The attorney actually makes more money per hour by settling your case favorably and efficiently, creating the ultimate win-win for the client and attorney. The longer your case takes, the less money the attorney makes per hour. They are now incentivized to work effectively, efficiently, and creatively on your case.

Results and efficiency

Have you ever wondered if your attorney is really working as diligently as they can to wrap up your case? Do you hate getting invoices that tell you the attorney spent 0.5 hours talking to the opposing counsel about discovery and disclosure requests? Do you wonder if they also talked about this weekend's plans or the upcoming convention they are both speaking at? With flat fees, you no longer get those annoying invoices. You no longer have to wonder if your attorney is spending too long on your case. The more efficient your attorney, the better! You are not paying by the minute.

Capped fee divorce

Capped fee divorce is just what it sounds like. The attorney works on an hourly basis but promises at the outset of the divorce not to exceed a certain cap. I don't have any personal experience with the capped fee divorce, but I can see how this option would be very beneficial to clients. They get the benefits of not overpaying for the number of hours an attorney spends, but also receive a guarantee that the fee will not exceed their given budget.

Notes

PART II

Chapter 3
How to File for Divorce

Many people want to know **how to get a divorce**, yet finding step-by-step instructions from actual qualified professionals is very difficult. We have found that our clients, and those who are representing themselves, all want more information and may have questions that their attorney has not answered.

The initial filings

Every case starts with either a Petition for Dissolution/Legal Separation or a Petition to Establish custody, paternity, and/or child support.

In a nutshell, you are either getting a divorce/separation/annulment or you have had a child with someone you are not married to and need to establish custody/ parenting time and/or child support.

For anyone going through these legal events, the same process must be followed. This section will describe the first step of your case, the initial documents. You will learn what to file, where to file, how to serve the opposing party and how to respond. I will offer tips on drafting and filing your documents and the path of least resistance to get your opposing party served. By doing the first step correctly, you help set yourself up for success.

First, determine what type of case you have:

- Divorce with Children
- Divorce without Children
- Covenant Marriage Divorce with Children
- Covenant Marriage Divorce without Children
- Legal Separation
- Annulment

- Initial Establishment of Legal Decision Making, Parenting Time, Paternity and Support (or any combination of the issues)

You will file a Petition for "(fill in any of the above case types that apply to you)" and all accompanying documents to start your case. If you have children and you are filing for Divorce, your Petition will be accompanied by a family court sensitive data sheet, a preliminary injunction, a notice of right to convert health insurance, an affidavit of minor children and a notice regarding creditors.

If you are filing a Petition without children, you will not need to provide the affidavit of minor children or the parent information program. Check in your county to find out the exact accompanying documents you will need. There is nothing more frustrating than driving to the courthouse, waiting in line, and getting the clerk to look at your documents only to have them rejected because you don't have a specific supplementary form required by the county.

Drafting the Petition

When drafting your Petition you have the option of being very specific, very vague, or somewhere in between. This is a strategic decision that depends on the facts of your specific case.

You may want to use vague language by asking for "an equitable distribution of property" or "reasonable parenting time to be determined by the parties" in order to leave yourself room to refine and change your position as you move through discovery. You may find through discovery that separate property exists that you were previously unaware of, or you may decide to sell the house, or you may exchange property for spousal maintenance, etc.

By keeping your initial documents vague, you can *avoid making inconsistent statements to the court* while refining your position and leaving yourself open to all possibilities. You should avoid making inconsistent statements to the court whenever possible. For instance, if you ask for $2500 per month spousal maintenance in your petition, $1200/month in your motion for temporary orders, and $3500 in your pre- trial statement, the judge is likely to be annoyed by this lack of consistent information. I have seen judges award attorney's fees against the inconsistent party. Being vague avoids this problem.

Another reason to keep some statements vague is to avoid inflaming or angering the opposing party. For instance, if things are quite amicable, and you and your spouse have talked through many details that you agree upon but you are still negotiating a spousal maintenance and child support number, consider stating only that you "may be eligible under the statute for spousal maintenance in an amount and duration to be determined," or ask for "child support to be ordered pursuant to the Arizona guidelines."

If you believe that your spouse or ex is unlikely to respond to your petition, then you must draft your petition very specifically. If an opposing party fails to respond to a petition, you become eligible to seek a default judgment against the party. You will be awarded everything in your petition—ONLY everything in your petition. For that reason, if an opposing party doesn't respond but you have failed to include a parenting plan in your petition, you must file an amended petition, serve the opposing party, and wait for the allotted time frame again.

There are some things you must include in your petition or you will be barred from changing your position. You must state whether or not significant domestic violence has occurred during the marriage. Do not omit this fact. If domestic violence has occurred, make sure to include it in your petition. This factor is pivotal in the decision of legal decision making and parenting time.

Similarly, if you and the other party agree on everything, you can arrange for a strategic default by crafting a petition specific to your agreement and one that addresses all outstanding issues. Then, the other party need not respond or pay the fee for responding. The Petitioner can seek a default judgment as a fast track way of getting divorced or getting a custody order entered.

While there is no need to use "legalese" when drafting your petition, you will want to make sure that you write in a clear way that lets the judge know what you are asking him or her to do. You do not need to say: "COMES NOW, Donald Duck, Petitioner of the land of Disney, to hereby request that henceforth he be granted sole legal decision making." But instead you could say something to the effect of: "Petitioner, Donald Duck, requests he be granted sole legal decision making." Then you can set out your reasons. Have a friend or family member edit your document and make sure it is written clearly. Grammatical or spelling errors are not uncommon and will have no actual effect on your case; it is more important that the substance of what you are asking for is clear and you have addressed all issues.

Filing the Petition

Your Petition must be notarized and for that reason is not eligible for e-filing in Maricopa County. (Not all counties have e-filing, so make sure and check with the local courts). You should take three or four copies of your documents with you to be stamped: one for you, one for your attorney (if you have one), one for the judge, and one for the opposing party. You should also expect to pay a filing fee when you file your petition. The filing fee in Maricopa County is $318 as of this writing.

If you are unable to physically take the Petition and accompanying documents to the courthouse, either because you don't drive or because you work business hours, you can hire a "runner" to take the documents for you. Many legal document preparer companies will facilitate the filing for you, or an attorney's office can facilitate the filing for you. When you get to the courthouse, you will go to the filing clerks and either take a number or wait in line. At the counter, the clerks will examine your paperwork to make sure everything is there. They will file stamp your documents, collect the fee, give you a case number, and assign a judge. You will then take one of your file stamped copies to the judge's box and deliver the document.

Service of the Petition

The day you serve the petition on the opposing party is a very important day. Not only does that trigger the time from which the opposing party must respond, it also "severs the community." That means any debts incurred or income earned after the service of the petition will be separate property and debt. You won't be divorced yet, but you are slightly less than married because you are free from the community property rules if you end up going through the divorce.

Along with the petition, the following documents must be served on the opposing party:

- "Family Court Cover Sheet"
- "Summons"
- "Preliminary Injunction"
- "Petition for Dissolution of Marriage (Divorce) With or Without Children"
- "Notice of Right to Convert Health Insurance"
- "Notice Regarding Creditors"

You may serve a party in a number of ways. The first and most preferable means of service is by **acceptance of service**. If the opposing party will sign an acceptance of service, service can be completed quickly and easily and without additional costs. Here is a letter/email that we regularly send in order to encourage an opposing party to accept service:

Dear Daisy,

Ms. Tarascio has been has hired by Donald Duck to assist with an annulment of marriage. I have paperwork for you that I would like to get to you. We would like to avoid both the cost and embarrassment associated with having you served via process server. We are hoping that you agree and will accept service of the documents.

Accepting service means you would need to provide us with a notarized copy of the attached Acceptance of Service, which acknowledges that you have received the documents only, not that you agree with them. You may access a **filed copy of the documents along with the acceptance of service** using the link provided.

Once you have acceptance of service, you generally have 20 days to respond if you are within the state of Arizona, and 30 days if you are outside of the state. In the event you are willing to accept service and need an extension, we can generally be very accommodating to your extension requests. If you are unwilling to accept service, we will need to hire a process server and we will seek reimbursement of those costs from you through the Court.

Please let me know as soon as possible if you are willing to accept service, or if you have any questions. While we cannot give you legal advice, we do keep a list of very reasonable attorneys who can give you a free consultation and will work toward a resolution without charging unreasonable fees. Having committed attorneys on both sides will result in faster resolution and lower overall fees. Let us know if you would like the list of attorneys.

Feel free to borrow whatever language is helpful in encouraging your opposing party to accept service. If they agree, you will need a notarized copy of the acceptance of service to file with the court. This serves as the "Notice of Service" and is essential for your court file.

In the event that acceptance of service isn't possible and the party is in Arizona, you can hire a **process server**. Process servers must be licensed in the state of Arizona, so you cannot have your brother, friend or neighbor serve the documents for you. You cannot serve the documents yourself either. Process servers generally charge between $40-$100 to serve documents depending on the person, how far they must travel, and how many attempts must be made.

Another alternative is having **the sheriff serve documents**. This is always an option if you are seeking to serve an order of protection; it may be possible for other documents as well.

Service via registered mail is also a viable form of service.

Sometimes a petitioner may not know the whereabouts of an opposing party. In that case, we must make every effort to locate the party by using a private investigator, social media, contacting relatives, etc. After we have exhausted these possibilities and still cannot find the party, we can ask the judge to allow **"alternative service."** Alternative service is most often **service by publication** in a newspaper. This takes weeks if not months and is not the preferred method of service, but it is an option when we have no other way of finding an opposing party.

No matter how we serve your opposing party, you must file a "notice of service" with the court to indicate how and when the opposing party was served.

Filing Your Response

If you have been served with a Petition inside Arizona, you have 20 days to respond. If you are located outside the state of Arizona, you have 30 days to respond. Receiving a Petition can be gut-wrenching, even when you knew it was coming. If you are blind-sided by a Petition, you are likely hurt, angry, scared and may be overwhelmed. It is easy to bury your head in the sand, but you can't! You must respond to the Petition.

When drafting your response, many attorneys use an **admit/deny** format. A response may be as simple as "I admit paragraphs 1-6. I deny paragraphs 7-12. I'd like to be awarded attorney's fees."

The problem with the admit/deny format is that you cannot read the response with- out the petition next to it. Your entire case is controlled by what the petitioner has written. Instead, I recommend writing your response as a counter petition, so that anyone can pick up your response and know exactly what you are asking for. Instead of stating, "I deny paragraph 12", consider saying "I disagree that the Petitioner should have sole legal decision making. Instead, Petitioner and Respondent should share joint legal decision-making. Both Petitioner and Respondent have always been active parts of the children's lives and should remain that way after divorce." Anyone reading your response to paragraph 12 knows what you want and why you want it.

Note: Many people ask if they should be the Petitioner or Respondent. There isn't really a right answer. There are advantages and disadvantages to both. As long as you know how to play to your case strengths, your status as Petitioner or Respondent should have no bearing on the outcome.

Motion for Temporary Orders

A motion for temporary orders may be filed with either the Petition or the Response, or any time after a Petition has been filed in a given case. The motion requests an expedited and temporary order on an issue while the case is ongoing. Since it may take a year or even more to secure a divorce, a temporary order can be a lifesaver if you need child support, spousal maintenance, you want to sell the house, or you need access to community property controlled by your spouse. In fact, you can get a temporary order for almost anything. Some people need a temporary order on where a child will go to school, a parenting time schedule, who will control the family business, etc. If you have a pressing issue that cannot wait, file a motion for temporary orders.

When drafting your motion for temporary orders, you cannot be vague. In this motion, you must tell the court specifically what you would like. This is particularly difficult when asking for spousal maintenance. You don't have the opposing party's Affidavit of Financial Information AFI (more on this later), which is a key document when determining how much to ask for. Consider asking that the opposing party pay certain bills and try to ask for only the cash that you need. Regardless of what you are asking the court to do, be specific about what you would like and why you need a temporary order.

E-filing

In Maricopa County many documents can be e-filed. This means you upload the document within the system and the clerk files the documents for you. (Not all counties have e-filing, so make sure and check with the local courts). It can usually take up to 24 hours after you have e-filed for it to be accepted by the court.

As of this writing, documents that are filed after the initial Petition and proof of service documents may be e-filed. That means you can e-file any motions, responses, notices, or replies.

Here are the instructions for how to e-file a document:

1. Set up your initial account here: https://efiling.clerkofcourt.maricopa.gov/fd-login.asp
2. Print and sign your document for filing. Scan and upload to your computer as a PDF.
3. Log in to your eFiling account and click "File Now."
4. Enter your Case Number and click "Confirm Case"; make sure that the Case Summary, shown in green, is for your case.

5. Click on "Browse" next to "Select Document" and find your PDF version of the document on your computer; double-click on it, or click on it once and then click "Open."

6. Scroll down the choices on "Select Filing Type" to find the most appropriate/applicable category for your document.

7. Fill in the "Document Title" using the COMPLETE name of your document (this will be on the right side of page one of your document, just under the Case Number).

8. Click on "Upload Document" and look for the words "You may submit this filing" in green. You should also see your document's title on the right side of the screen.

9. Click on the "Complete Filing" button, and it should take you to a new screen labeled "Confirm Your Filing." Verify the information, and click "Submit Filing." This should take you to a "Filing Complete" screen.

10. Print the confirmation page of the filing and mail with your document (if not required to be served pursuant to applicable rules of procedure, etc.) to the opposing party or counsel.

Sometimes there are filing fees associated with the documents that you have to file. In that event you will receive an email from the clerk stating exactly how much is owed and for which document. Only after you have paid the filing fee will the clerk actually file stamp and accept your document. Regardless of whether a fee is owed, you will receive an email from the clerk once your document has been accepted. At that point you will be able to access the document via the electronic court record (ECR), which we will talk about next. You can then print the documents with the file stamp and send a copy to the opposing party.

E-filing can save you much time and money by avoiding the costs of sending a runner to the court, avoiding actually traveling to the court, waiting in line, and filing your documents in person.

Electronic Court Record ("ECR") Account

The ECR is another great example of how technology can make life easier and more convenient. It allows you access to all documents filed with the court in your case. The ECR is available for all documents filed since 2005, and all probate cases dating from

1997. ECR access is not available for juvenile cases, legal support staff, and pro hac vice. Registration is easy and simple; however, an Arizona driver's license is required. It is important to note that the ECR and eFile systems are separate and require separate registrations. If you are not currently using the ECR, you can create an account by following the instructions on the link below:

https://ecr.clerkofcourt.maricopa.gov/Registration.aspx

Once you add a case to ECR you can access documents for that case by clicking on the case. Your screen will then show the lists of court documents in the top half and preview the documents in the bottom half. The preview toolbar allows you to download and print the document.

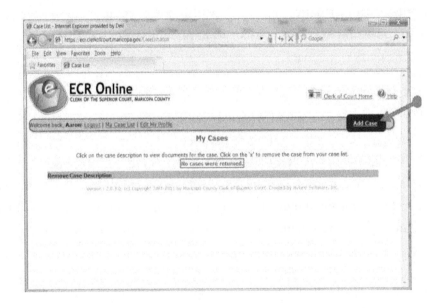

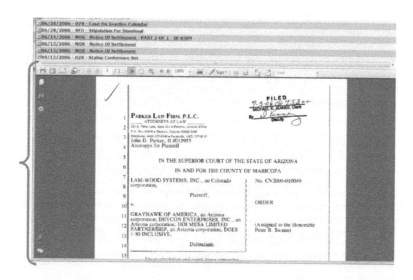

IMPORTANT: The Preview feature requires Adobe Acrobat reader. If you don't have Adobe Acrobat Reader, you can download it here for free:

https://get.adobe.com/reader/

If you ever need help navigating the ECR, you can reach the ECR technical support team at:

Phone: (602) 372-5375 (press #2 > press #6 > press #4)

E-mail: ecr@cosc.maricopa.gov

Default

The amount of time you must wait in order to file for default depends on the waiting period for the particular type of documents you filed. For instance, even though the opposing party must respond within 20 days (if you're in Arizona) to your petition for dissolution, there is a 60-day waiting period in Arizona from the date of service until you can actually get a divorce.

If no response has been filed by the deadline, then you can request a default hearing. In order to have the hearing set, file an affidavit of default. You need only mail or hand-deliver one copy of your affidavit of default to the other party. See the time- table below for the various times the other party must wait. If the last day falls on a weekend or holiday, then the following business day will be the day when you can file the default papers. You will need to serve the opposing party with the default paperwork and they have an additional 10-day grace period within which they can file a response.

DEFAULT TIMETABLE		
SERVICE BY	COUNT	EVENT
"Acceptance of Service" (in Arizona)	24 days	after other party signs "Acceptance of Service"
Process Server (in Arizona)	24 days	after other party receives papers from process server
Sheriff (in Arizona)	24 days	after other party receives papers from sheriff
"Acceptance of Service" (out of State)	34 days	after other party signs "Acceptance of Service"
Registered mail (out of State)	34 days	after other party signs green card
Process Server (out of State)	34 days	after other party receives papers from process server
Sheriff (out of State)	34 days	after other party receives papers from sheriff
Sheriff (out of State)	34 days	after other party receives papers from sheriff
Publication	64 days	after the 1st day of publication

After the 10-day grace period has passed, you can call the court to schedule your default hearing. In Maricopa County you can schedule the hearing online. Make sure to have your pleadings ready because they will want to know information like your case number and date of service.

For your default hearing, you (and several dozen other litigants who will have their hearing in the same session) will need to bring:

- Three copies of your proposed decree
- Three copies of an Order of Assignment
- The certificate that states you've attended the required parenting class
- Three copies of your proposed signed parenting plan
- Three copies of a completed child support worksheet.
- Support worksheet

- Wage information for both parties (if you have it) to support your child support worksheet numbers
- A 9 x 12 envelope addressed to the other party, stamped with three standard postage stamps
- A copy of any prior child support orders
- A birth certificate for each of your children

You will be seated in the courtroom on the day of your hearing, along with the others who are waiting for their default decree. When it is your turn, the judge will call the case by stating your last name and that of the opposing party. The judge will examine the petition and the other paperwork you have brought. She will be looking to make sure the petition matches the proposed decree. She may ask you questions and may even make changes to your decree.

On one occasion a mother was asking that the court order joint legal decision-making. After the judge asked the mother some questions she determined that the father was currently in jail for assaulting the mother. Since the statute required the judge not order joint legal decision-making when there was significant domestic violence, the judge signed the decree awarding sole legal decision-making to the mother.

Changing Judges

Once the judge is assigned to your case, I recommend you do some research on the judge. Find out how he or she rules or has ruled in the past on issues similar to yours. Go online and join forums to see if you can determine a judge's philosophy on issues you're facing.

Judges do things differently from one another. They have different opinions, biases, and preferences, and different ways of doing things. They are, after all, asked to make judgments based on their application of the laws to your situation. While this seems obvious, you do have the ability to change judges one time, as a matter of right, before the judge has made a ruling based on the Arizona Rules of Family Law Procedure.

Some people want their issue to be handled as quickly as possible. Some judges move cases along as quickly as they can and actively manage their calendars and cases.

Others wait to even set a trial until the parties have exchanged all information and they indicate to the court they are ready for a trial. Some judges have preferences on school choice issues, parenting time schedules, how they feel about the right of first refusal, etc. Some judges are very strict about deadlines; others will allow almost everything to come into evidence.

If you decide to change judges, you need only file a "notice of the change of judge." This is not discretionary and it will be granted. This has a practical effect of slowing down your case, which can be advantageous or not depending on your circumstances.

Practically speaking, we're talking about matchmaking cases and personalities. Changing judges means you are rolling the dice again. You can't elect the judge you want. In the event you cannot find enough information online, or from friends, you can either sit in the judge's courtroom to hear how she or she rules, or you can talk to a local attorney. One of the benefits of an attorney is the history of going before a judge many times and learning their personalities and preferences.

Notes

Chapter 4
Disclosure and Discovery

Now is when we really start thinking like a divorce lawyer

This next phase in your case will help you to develop your positions and move toward settlement or trial. If you do this part of your case correctly, the following phases of negotiations and trial become much easier. Without taking this phase seriously, negotiations and trial could be disastrous.

Going through a family court case, means one or more aspects of your life is in turmoil. There are incidents that happen every day that cause you stress, mess with your emotions, and cost you financially. Perhaps the most difficult part of representing yourself is determining what is legally relevant versus what is emotionally relevant.

We have already discussed that Arizona is a no-fault divorce state. That means your spouse's bad behavior, which has left you feeling hurt and betrayed, may not be legally relevant to the judge. In family law, determining what is and isn't relevant to the judge can be a difficult task for attorneys since we are dealing with issues like "the best interests of the children," which is not exactly a concrete concept. For some- one living in the midst of turmoil it can be next to impossible. That your spouse is an abusive alcoholic is certainly legally relevant to child custody issues, but if your spouse is a chronic cheater, it's not necessarily relevant to child support, but may be relevant to property division. This section will help determine what is legally relevant to your positions and how you need to prove it.

What is Evidence?

Evidence can be witness testimony or documents and other physical sources of in- formation like photos. You must offer evidence for every element of every issue relevant to your case.

Rules of Evidence

In family court, the rules of evidence are relaxed unless one party files a "notice of strict compliance." Under the relaxed rules, all relevant evidence is generally admissible unless it is repetitive or abusive. Generally, if it is relevant to the issues, a Judge will allow you to use the evidence. If a notice of strict compliance is filed, all of the rules of evidence including hearsay and authentication rules apply. If you are going up against an attorney and they have filed the notice, we suggest you seek advice from an attorney. He or she can help you properly prepare your evidence for submission to the court.

In the two to four months following your initial filings, you will need to identify, compile and organize your evidence. This is a daunting task even for some attorneys, so here, I will give you step by step instructions for what to do.

Identify What You Must Disclose and Evidence that You Need

When you argue your case in front of the judge, the judge will look at each legal issue one at a time. Your job will be to apply your specific facts to the existing law. When a judge decides the outcome of your case, it will be issue by issue. For issues such as legal decision-making and parenting time, they are required to make "findings of fact and conclusions of law." We must keep this in mind when identifying potential evidence and later determining the evidence we will use to prove our case.

The first step in tackling this phase is to figure out what legal issues are relevant to your case, determined the legal elements within the issue, and the corresponding evidence that you need or that you have.

Potential legal issues in the case include:

- Property division
- Debt division
- Alimony or spousal maintenance
- Child support
- Child custody legal decision-making
- Parenting time
- Attorney fees

- Enforcement
- Modification

Start by identifying which issues are relevant in your case. Then look at the substantive law for each issue to determine which elements must be proven. Once you know the elements that you must prove, then you can identify what piece of evidence is necessary to establish a basis for each element.

For example, if child support is a relevant issue to your case, we will look at the child support calculator or read the statute regarding what is necessary to determine child support.

We will find that, at a minimum, to determine child-support you need to agree upon or prove the following elements:

1. The names and ages of the minor children.
2. How much income does each party earn?
3. Who provides health insurance for the children and what is the cost?
4. Do the children attend childcare? If so, what is the cost and who pays for it?
5. Do the children have any extraordinary needs for expenses?

Then for each of the five elements we have listed above, we can determine whether witness testimony or documents will be used to prove our position. If we start from the very beginning of our case thinking like a lawyer, and organizing our documents and evidence around elements of the issues, it will help us to filter out things that are happening in your day-to-day life that will not be relevant to the judge.

Continuing with our example, for element number one, witness testimony will establish the names and ages the minor children. This is almost never in dispute and almost never requires documentation.

For element number two, incomes of the parties, proving this element can be simple or complex. Usually, each party's affidavit of financial information will be sufficient to prove income of the parties. We will talk in depth about the affidavit of financial information later.

Element number three should be fairly simple to prove, using insurance statements, insurance cards, and paychecks or bank statements to prove the cost of insuring the children.

Element number four relates to childcare. Be prepared to prove where the children attend childcare and how much you pay for it receipts, a written statement from a witness/your childcare provider, you may need a calendar to show the days and times the children attended childcare if this issue is in dispute.

The same analysis applies to element number five. If your children have exceptional expenses or needs, be prepared to show that they have these exceptional needs, why the additional expenses are necessary, why your spouse or ex should help you pay for them.

How to Put Together Your File

Many people have different ways of organizing a legal file. One popular way is to break down a file into pleadings, court orders or minute entries, correspondence with the opposing party, and disclosures.

While there is nothing wrong with that approach, and it may work for you, I am advocating a different approach.

When organizing your disclosures, keep the end in mind.

At a minimum, have one folder for each legal issue (depending on the size and complexity of the issues, you may need subfolders for each element of each issue). As time goes on and new evidence unfolds (like emails from your ex saying he got a new job making $100k) you can determine which element of which issue the email is relevant to and put it in the proper file or folder.

You will also need a folder for pleadings and orders, but by organizing everything else in relation to how the judge thinks, you can stay focused and save time when preparing for trial.

How to Identify Witnesses

In most Arizona counties, you will be given very little time to prove your case. Because of that, use of witness testimony is usually kept to a minimum, but it can make or break a case. You will need witness testimony if your testimony is not sufficient on the issue or element of the issue, and there is no documentation to prove what you are trying to establish.

A witness can be anyone with personal knowledge on a relevant issue. A grandparent or friend could be a witness to an incident of domestic violence. An employer could be a witness on anticipated future income.

What about Expert Witnesses

Expert witnesses are people with special training or knowledge who are asked to give their opinion on a given issue. Expert witnesses like parenting coordinators, court appointed advisors, or forensic psychologists are often used to provide opinions and facts surrounding issues related to parenting time and legal decision making. They are most often appointed by the court, so there is no need to worry about disclosures.

The other type of expert witness frequently used in family law cases are financial experts. A financial expert may be used to testify about the value of certain assets, or the earning capacity of a spouse, or the value of a family-owned business. These experts are you usually hired by one of the parties or hired jointly to render an opinion. If you hire a financial expert or any expert witness that the court is unaware of, you must disclose the name, credentials, and subject matter the expert will testify about 60 days prior to trial. Sometimes you need only the report of the expert and you do not need them to actually appear in court and testify.

There are certain types of cases that are very difficult to prove without an expert.

- If your case involves domestic violence and you don't have direct evidence of that violence, you should consider hiring an expert or asking that the court appoint an expert for you.
- If your case involves suspected parental alienation syndrome, these are very difficult to prove, and you will need an expert.

- If you suspect your spouse has a mental illness but it is undocumented, you will need a psychological evaluation to prove the mental illness exists.
- If your case involves a business and it must be valued, you will need a business valuator to render an opinion of value.
- If you have already had a temporary order, presented evidence on an issue such as spousal maintenance, and received an unfavorable order, consider hiring an expert witness to offer different facts or back up your claims, at the next hearing.
- If your case involves separate and community property, co-mingled funds, or other complicated financial issues, consider hiring an expert witness.

This is by no means an exhaustive list, just examples for your consideration. Once you have identified each issue and the corresponding elements, and you have determined the evidence that exists for each element, you can evaluate the strength of evidence that you have and consider what role witnesses will play.

Given the framework, we can now dive in to disclosures and discovery.

Rule 49 of the Arizona Family Law Rules of Procedure lays out what you are **required** to disclose even without the other party asking for the documents and even if you do not intend to use the documents as evidence. In reality, self-represented litigants rarely follow all of the rules and rarely disclose everything that they need to under rule 49. Rule 49 can help you identify what might be important and what you may need to get from the opposing party.

Thankfully, it is also broken down by legal issues.

Mandatory Disclosures

In Arizona, evidence that is not properly disclosed cannot be used in trial. This means that if you do not follow the correct process for disclosing your evidence, the Judge may refuse to look at what you bring to trial despite all your hard work identifying, organizing, and preparing your evidence. This can be devastating and could mean losing on very important issues like child support or parenting time. It could mean you walk away with less than half of the community property. *You could literally lose on every single issue, if you do not take this part of the process seriously and approach it with diligence.*

Disclosure simply means that you have provided the opposing party a copy of the evidence you intend use. You may find it easier to organize your documents within online files. We do much of our disclosure within the law firm electronically to the opposing parties as well.

Disclosure statements are required under the rules and simply act as a guideline and cover page for your disclosures. Within the statement, you will identify the names of the documents, your position on the relevant legal issues, the names and addresses of any witnesses you intend call, and a summary of what you anticipate they will testify to. It can feel very counterintuitive to tell the opposing party exactly what you plan to present to the court. However, it's not only required under the rules, it should also help you to reach settlement. The idea is that if your ex knows how strong your case is for child support there is simply no need to litigate the issue.

Completing and filing a disclosure statements also puts the court on notice what you have disclosed and when. This prevents the opposing party for making false claims they have not received your disclosures.

You do not have to file your disclosure statements, but you can. <u>You do not file the documents you are disclosing</u>. They are simply given to the opposing party. Your first disclosure statement is due to the opposing party within 40 days after the response has been filed. You may complete several disclosure statements throughout your case since the duty to disclose is ongoing.

The Doctrine of "Clean Hands"

There is a legal defense known as the doctrine of "clean hands." It can be most easily translated as "S/he did it too" (insert bratty voice here). Anyone who has children or who has been around children is familiar with the commonly used defense.

Johnny comes to you looking for vindication and says: "Suzy took my blanket and she won't give it back!" You talk to Suzy who says "But he took my doll!"

This scenario plays out in courts all over the country with a slightly different variation of the facts. The clean hands defense most recently reared its head in a case I was involved in regarding hidden income.

I represented Father. We believed that Mother was hiding thousands of dollars in rental income each month, which should be factored into Father's child support obligation. Mother owned two homes, a rental and the home where she resided. We believed the rental property was owned free and clear and the residential home carried a mortgage. Mother simply stated she had a net rental income of $50/month. She refused to supply the mortgage documents.

We started our pursuit of discovery with a letter to the opposing counsel requesting clarification on the subject and reminding him that the documents and questions we were asking were well within the mandatory disclosures required under rule 49.

When we did not receive an answer to the letter, we sent uniform and non-uniform family law interrogatories clearly and unequivocally requesting that Mother supply us with each property she owned, what was owed on each property, who lived in the property, and a rental agreement for any rental property.

While Mother responded to many of the questions within the interrogatories, she did not answer the questions regarding her properties. At this point, we are very close to proving our allegations that she had the additional income. Our next step was to file a motion to compel.

This motion asked the court to compel Mother to hand over the information and answer the interrogatory. If it is granted, attorney's fees are mandatory, meaning Mother would have to pay Father's attorneys fees associated with the discovery attempts.

On the day of the hearing, we set out to make our case on both the rental income and why Mother should pay Father's attorney fees due to her failure to comply with the rules and respond to our reasonable requests. Father offered testimony about why he believed Mother was hiding income and why she had acted unreasonably and cost him additional attorneys fees. We had planned well and executed our strategy and the Judge seemed to be aligning with our position. Then Mother's attorney began cross-examination of the Father. The last question he asked was: "Isn't it true you also have rental income that you have failed to disclose?" It was clear from Father's face that he did, indeed, have rental income he failed to disclose. Father attempted to explain that it was only very recently acquired, and, it was only a minimal amount of rental income. But the damage was done. The Judge stated he would use both parties income from their AFI. Father would not get attorneys fees and Mother would not be imputed the additional rental income in the child support calculation.

What is the moral of the story? It is essential that you comply with the rules of procedure in family court. Unfortunately, if you miss something, or fail to comply with the rules, the opposing party may use it as a defense. In this case, my client spent thousands of dollars perusing information and attorneys fees. His failure to mention $30 in rental income on his updated AFI, cost him thousands of dollars in overpaid child support and attorneys fees.

Our duty to disclose is ongoing. If something changes, you must disclose.

The Affidavit of Financial Information

The most important and non-negotiable mandatory disclosure is the Affidavit of Fi- nancial Information (AFI). If your case involves child support, spousal maintenance or attorneys fees, you and your ex will need to submit a completed and accurate AFI. This is one of the only disclosure documents that must be filed with the court.

It is very important that the information you put on your affidavit of financial information is accurate. Within the document you will need to identify your house- hold budget, your sources of income, your debts, your assets. We have broken the task down into a three-step process.

Step 1-Assess Income

The first step is to evaluate the total amount of income of the spouses. If one or both people work at salaried positions, this is fairly straightforward.

Calculating income can be more challenging, however, if the other spouse is self-employed without a set monthly income. Income from sources other than employment, such as trust funds, retirement accounts, government benefits, and royalties should also be assessed.

For several aspects of a divorce, including child support and spousal maintenance, it's imperative to know the income each spouse receives. If you still have access to the house and all of the documents and accounts, it is very important that you get this information.

Go through the house and identify all of the information you possibly can. Identify where the accounts are held, the user names and passwords, statements, W2s, tax returns, 1099s etc.

Step 2-Document Income

Start Printing! There is no telling how long these accounts will be open. Print bank statements, copy W2s, tax returns, profit and loss statements etc.

For the self-employed spouse, it includes additional documents such as bank ac- count and credit card statements, business records, and loan applications.

Determining the income of a self-employed person is not always simple, but having access to the appropriate documents can make it much easier. Once a spouse moves out, gaining access to those documents can diminish or even disappear.

Step 3-Create a Budget

After income has been assessed and documented, the final step in figuring out the financial situation involves creating a current and prospective budget. The budget should detail your income and expenses both currently and what you anticipate them to be in the future (if you are married and getting a divorce). The same pains- taking detail used in documenting income should be applied here in gathering bills, financial statements, and other documents that show the family's expenses. This is much easier to do while living in the home and without the possibility of anyone hiding assets or information.

You will use the Affidavit of Financial Information (AFI) to state both current and future anticipated expenses. This requires planning!

This budget can be critically important in determining how much spousal maintenance will eventually be paid or received. The laborious work of creating a thorough budget is well worth the effort, and proving the accuracy of the budget with documents is even more valuable in terms of preventing further conflict.

Consider the free tool Mint.com to help you organize your information and assist with the creation of an accurate budget.

The AFI requires asset and debt information as well, however, those sections of the AFI are more important in a divorce than in an action to establish custody for un- married parents or in a modification.

If property division is an issue (because you are going through a divorce), you will need to identify your assets.

You should itemize all of the assets on a spreadsheet (use Mint.com for a free resource to build your asset picture), detailing the date the asset was purchased, the purchase price, and the estimated current value.

For some assets, such as the home, this is fairly straightforward, while other assets will be more difficult to assess. It's unlikely that most people have kept records of the purchase date and price of every piece of furniture, collectible, and other home furnishing they own.

It's important to make as complete an itemization as possible, however, and don't forget to also check the contents of any self-storage facilities or safety deposit boxes.

If you don't have access to information, we will use the discovery tools to request the information from the opposing party.

There are four categories of assets to consider:

- Marital residence and other real estate including lots, vacation homes, cabins, etc.
- Intangible assets, such as financial and retirement accounts, stocks, bonds, etc.
- Business interests.
- Personal Property, including physical assets, such as furniture, artwork, vehicles, etc.

In addition to identifying the assets, you will need to identify the debts.

If you have more than a few debts, you will want to itemize debts on the spreadsheet, detailing the amount of principal owed, interest rate, creditor, and account numbers.

There are five categories of debts to consider:

- Mortgages, equity loans and other debts secured by real estate
- Auto loans and other debts secured by physical assets
- Credit cards, including store-specific cards and gas cards
- Student loans
- Tax liabilities

Some of the records and documents to photocopy or scan:

- Tax returns
- Pay stubs
- Statements for all financial and retirement accounts
- Statements for all loans and credit cards
- Vehicle titles
- Photographs of physical assets, such as china, crystal, artwork, furniture, computers, etc.

This can be a time-consuming task, but time spent copying supporting records and creating a thorough itemization will be a huge advantage down the road.

It's common for the one spouse to have limited access to the marital residence and its contents after moving out, which allows assets to disappear or be damaged.

The itemization will also prevent additional unscrupulous and unethical behavior on the part of the other spouse, and it will y by reducing the work to be done by a lawyer who bills for his or her time.

While you are gathering all this information to complete the AFI, it still represents potential evidence, so you will want to file it away in the appropriate folders within the relevant legal issue.

Some evidence will be relevant to more than one legal issue. In that case, I recommend making a few copies of the evidence and placing all relevant evidence in each section of your disclosure/discovery folders.

Additionally, you will want to document what you have received and when from the opposing party. You could add a tab to your spreadsheet or simply create a separate folder for what your ex has disclosed and when. You can then take a copy of any- thing relevant to your issues and place them in the corresponding folder.

What if you don't have the information you need?

What if you have done all this work, you have dutifully disclosed and created dis- closure statements and your ex refuses to give you anything! This happens all the time, even when people are represented by attorneys. So, what can you do to get the information you need?

First, you can send a letter requesting the information you need and pointing out the mandatory disclosure rules in the Arizona Rules of Family Law Procedure.

Next, you can use the discovery tools to formally demand your ex give you what you need. With most of the tools below, the opposing party will have 40 days to respond to your requests.

Finally, if you still don't have what you need, you can consider filing a motion to compel. Before you are allowed to file the motion to compel you must make a "good faith effort" to resolve the discovery dispute. That means even after you have 1) asked nicely 2) provided discovery requests and 3) waited 40 days, you must still ask again before filing your motion to compel. This could mean you make a call, send an email or write a letter giving your ex a final deadline before filing your motion to compel.

If after all of that, your ex still won't comply and the motion to compel is granted, you will also be awarded your attorney's fees. It is mandatory and not discretionary. If you are representing yourself, I suggest you request monetary sanctions, which is the equivalent of your ex paying your attorney's fees. This sort of bad behavior should be punished. You can't have a fair fight if one side won't play by the rules.

Additionally, the rules are designed to put everyone on an even playing field, working with the same information in order to achieve a fair result. If you can't get information, it's difficult to settle a case, forcing you to spend more of your precious resources in the emotional abyss of a family law case.

What are the available "discovery tools"

You will notice that not everything is covered by the mandatory disclosure rule 49. There may be things you want that your ex is not required to disclose. Use the discovery tools to request anything even remotely relevant to your issues. Which tool you use depends on what you are requesting.

Note: *These legal documents do not get filed with the court.*

Interrogatories

Interrogatories, a frequently used and useful discovery tool, are questions that must be responded to in writing by the opposing party within 40 days of receipt. This locks in the answer of the opposing party and provides valuable information you can use in making your case. You can send both uniform and non-uniform interrogatories to the opposing party. As an example, the uniform interrogatories ask for the party to list all bank accounts, assets, insurance policies, pending litigation claims, etc. If your case has hotly contested issues, consider using the uniform interrogatories as a fantastic discovery tool for your case. The answers are almost ALWAYS useful.

Request for Production of Documents

Like the interrogatories, a Request for Production of Documents asks that the other party deliver to you the documents/things you are requesting within 40 days of receipt. You can ask for any and all relevant documents including Quickbooks files, criminal convictions, drug tests, and even medical records. You can also ask for a computer or tablet to have a forensic evaluator search for money or evidence of crimes like child pornography or drug dealing. This is a fantastic tool to accompany interrogatories.

Request for Admissions

Requests for admissions are used less frequently than the two tools above, but can provide valuable information and insight for less money than the cost of a deposition. In a request for admissions, the opposing party is asked admit/deny questions and must either admit or deny the questions that you ask. If they don't answer the requests within 40 days, they are automatically deemed to have "admitted" within the documents.

Depositions

Arguably, depositions are the most powerful discovery tool available to you as a litigant. A deposition allows you to ask any question that you would like of the opposing party (with few exceptions) under oath and on the record. This gives you the ability to test out questions and determine the opposing party's demeanor and ability to answer difficult questions. It also locks down their story. You can depose both parties and witnesses by serving a "Notice of Deposition" upon the party or witness(es) you intend to call. Then, you will want to schedule a court reporter to take the deposition. Give yourself enough time to get the written transcript well before trial.

Subpoena

A subpoena allows you to get documents from third parties such as banks, or command a witness to attend a hearing. A subpoena must be issued by the clerk of the court and served upon the intended recipient.

Each discovery tool can help you to achieve a given objective. As always, know your strategy and what you must prove to determine which tools to use. Consider the cost benefit analysis of each decision and take advantage of either a certified legal document preparer, lay legal advocate, or an attorney for further information.

What happens if you don't follow the rules? Here are two client stories related to the disclosure and discovery issues for you to consider.

A client story – undisclosed assets

The client had been married for 30 years. She had raised and home-schooled four children and helped build and manage the family business that supported them. She had been a committed and devoted Wife. The "baby" was 10 and still at home along with his sister who was a senior in high school. Honestly, Dad didn't seem all that interested in the kids anyway. He was leading a double life. His online dating profile stated he was 10 years younger and earned $500k/year – twice as much as he actually earned running their dental practice.

We had been working together for a year on her very complicated divorce. She had received her divorce decree, but items were missing. The judge failed to divide all of the property! She was devastated. She just wanted to be done! We had two options: appeal or motion for a new trial on the property issues and ask that the Judge simply divide the assets. We did the latter and the Judge granted a new trial. Ugh. This was not ideal.

In the meantime, we kept digging. This is when we found huge amounts of undis-closed accounts. While the Husband was claiming he had no money to pay child support and spousal maintenance, he was actually sitting on $100k in a hidden bank account!

So, what happens when you find hidden money? First, you get an emergency order freezing the funds so they cannot be spent by your lying, cheating, no good, dirty, rotten spouse.

Then, you prove at trial that the funds were undisclosed. Because we had done our job and affirmatively played by the rules disclosing everything, and we had sent discovery requests followed by letters requesting all documents, we are given ALL of the money.

That's right. When one spouse hides money during a divorce we can open the case and be awarded all- not just the community portion of the money.

It was a good day and a great victory for my client.

Notes

Chapter 5
Phase 2 - Prehearing Conference

After your initial filings and while you are conducting your discovery and disclosures, you will be set for prehearing conferences. Prehearing conferences, for the purposes of this section, are any court ordered judicial or quasi-judicial proceedings before your final evidentiary hearing or trial.

Their purpose is to determine the outstanding issues, lock in any settlements, and determine what, if any, assistance the court or the parties need in order to either reach an agreement or have a trial on the merits of the case.

Prehearing conferences set the tone for the case and determine many of the re- sources that will be used. We will also discuss any of the court-appointed advisers, or other court appointed experts that may be used in any given case.

Prehearing conferences consist of:

- Resolution management conferences
- Early resolution conferences
- Return hearings
- Status conferences
- Open negotiations
- Temporary orders hearings

Resolution management conference

A resolution management conference, or RMC, is set by the court in virtually every initial case. The RMC is a non-evidentiary hearing, which means that the judge should not look at exhibits or hear testimony, nor should they make rulings on any issues. This takes place in the judge's assigned courtroom. At the RMC, you and the opposing party will go before your assigned Judge and present your positions on all of the outstanding issues. You will file an RMC statement before the scheduled RMC and provide a copy to the opposing party. This statement is to be completed without argument and without emotion if possible. Since this is your first time in front of the judge and you will want to make a good first impression. Your RMC statement might say something like:

> "Legal Decision Making: Mother should be awarded sole legal decision-making because Father has been convicted of selling narcotics and domestic violence including assault."

You should add enough to back up your position, but nothing more and without a graphic description.

The RMC will be set for 30 minutes in front of your assigned judge. The judge will have read both of your RMC statements and will likely state whether or not there are issues that you both agree upon.

For instance, if both parties have stated that they would like joint legal decision-making, the judge will most likely ask the two of you to stand, raise your right hand, and put your agreement on the record. When you do this you are entering a "rule 69 agreement." It is binding and issue will never come up again. It is also possible that the two of you will enter into temporary agreements. That could be a temporary agreement that Father will continue to pay the mortgage and the car payment and Mother will continue to pay all of the utilities and the cell phone.

If there are no agreements to be reached the judge will either:

1. Set a final evidentiary hearing date.
2. Send the parties to a parenting conference or mediation.
3. Appoint a third-party to offer the court evidence on a specific outstanding issue.

If you would like the intervention of a third-party, because you are asking for drug testing or a psychological evaluation, the RMC statement is a great place to make the judge aware of your request. The judge may order what you're asking for or may request that you file a motion asking the court for ruling on your request.

Sometimes judges set an RMC on temporary orders. This is very confusing. It means that the judgment may or may not take evidence on any temporary orders request and may or may not enter orders regarding temporary issues. Sometimes a judge will have an RMC on temporary orders only to set a temporary orders hearing at a later date. If this happens, call the JA, or judicial assistant, and see if you can find out whether or not the judge would like to take evidence at the RMC. If you cannot find out in advance, be prepared for either possibility.

Early Resolution Conference (ERC)

An early resolution conference may be set instead of, or in addition to, an RMC. An early resolution conference is only set if one or both parties are unrepresented by attorneys. It will not be scheduled if two attorneys are on the case.

The ERC takes place at the courthouse but not in a courtroom. It is scheduled for three hours and is facilitated by a mediator, not a judge. The mediator cannot make rulings, even if they want to. Temporary orders or final agreements will only be locked down if both parties agree. If you have been scheduled for an ERC, consider bringing an attorney with you. The combination of a law-trained mediator and an attorney has been very successful in nailing down favorable agreements for the represented party.

Unlike an RMC, where you do not need to bring or present evidence, <u>you will want to bring all of your evidence to the ERC</u>. If you can show the other party and the mediator the extent of your assets, income, and debts, it becomes much easier to persuade the opposing party to agree to your position.

If you do come to agreements, the mediator will draft those agreements, get each of your signatures, and take the agreement to a judge to be signed that day. It is possible to complete your entire case at the ERC.

Status Conference

A status conference is usually set by the judge at the RMC to take place following a certain event. For instance, if the judge sends two parents to mediation on a certain date, it isn't unusual for the judge to set a status conference for the following week. A judge may avoid scheduling a final evidentiary hearing until after both a mediation and a status conference have taken place. A status conference can either be telephonic or in person, and is usually set for 15 minutes. The purpose is simply to update the court on any progress that has been made or changes that have taken place and to decide the next step.

Return Hearings

Another prehearing conference that you may come across is a return hearing. A return hearing is sometimes set instead of an RMC in a post-decree, or modification case. There is no need to file any documents prior to the return hearing, although you may want to prepare some notes for yourself. The return hearing is a hybrid between the RMC and the status conference. It is not quite as informal as a status conference, nor is it as formal as an RMC. It usually takes place in a courtroom and is not typically conducted telephonically.

Open Negotiations

Opening negotiations are a new type of prehearing conference that takes place in- stead of the RMC. Attorneys are not allowed to attend open negotiations, where a Judge may ask questions of both parties to tease out positions and try to guide the parties to some agreements. If the Open Negotiation is unsuccessful, the Judge will simply proceed with the case as he/she would following an RMC.

Temporary Orders Hearings

Temporary orders hearings are only set if one of the parties files a motion for temporary orders. Even then, a hearing may not be set until after an RMC. It can take anywhere from 30 to 90 days to get in front of the judge for a temporary orders hearing. This hearing is unlike the others that we have discussed, because it is an evidentiary area hearing. That means the judge will take testimony, exhibits, and make rulings on the outstanding temporary issues.

To prepare for a temporary orders hearing, you need to gather evidence that sup- ports your position and prepare your testimony. This topic is covered more in the last chapter and in the chapter on preparing for trial.

A temporary orders hearing is usually scheduled for 30 minutes or 60 minutes so there is rarely time for any additional witnesses. The petitioner will present evidence first. The respondent will have the ability to cross-examine any witnesses called by the petitioner. Then the respondent will present their own case, and the petitioner we'll cross-examine any witnesses called by the respondent. Sometimes the judge will rule "from the bench," which means the Judge will deliver the verdict immediately and orally. More common however, is that the Judge will take the matter "under advisement." This means the ruling will be issued within 30 days in writing in what is called a minute entry.

A temporary order will give you an idea of how the judge is leaning on any given is- sue. It can be a trial run and could make you better prepared for a final evidentiary area hearing.

Court appointed intervention after the initial filing but before the final evidentiary hearing could include:

- Parenting conferences
- A psychological evaluation
- A comprehensive family evaluation/assessment
- A limited family evaluation/Assessment
- Reunification therapy
- Court appointed adviser

Parenting Conferences

A parenting conference is frequently scheduled when you have two good parents who don't agree on a parenting plan or there are concerns regarding parental fitness or addiction issues. Typically, the judge will order the parents to attend a parent conference at RMC. You will receive an order identifying the parenting conference provider and you will have 10 days to contact the provider and arrange the first ap- pointment. The parenting conference costs each party $300. The parent conference provider will review any collateral information that you have about the other party like emails, police reports, CPS reports, etc. The provider may even speak with third party witnesses.

A meeting is then scheduled for the parents, and the children if they are old enough, to speak with the provider. The conference provider acts like a cross between a mediator and an expert witness. The meeting is non-confidential and the provider will create a report for the court's review. The Parents are encouraged to come to agreements, which are written down by the provider and treated like a Rule 69 agreement. For many children, this is their opportunity to be heard on any opinions regarding what living arrangement they would like.

After the provider has reviewed the information, spoken with witnesses, and met with the parties and children, they will provide a written report to the parties and court. This can take up to 60 days. The report can contain any concerns they have about either parent or the children. Sometimes the provider will point out an issue the parents aren't even thinking about like a child's eating habits, or school attendance issues. Sometimes the parenting conference provider will recommend a psychological evaluation for either mother or father, or they may recommend alcohol or drug testing.

The judge will certainly read the report and rely on information within it. Most of the time judges adopt the recommendations and findings of the parenting conference provider. With that being said, you can use the reports to craft a settlement agreement or change your strategy moving forward in court.

Comprehensive Family Assessment/Comprehensive Evaluation

A comprehensive family assessment or a comprehensive evaluation can be ordered for many different reasons. Most often when a Judge suspects domestic violence, substance abuse, serious mental illness, or child abuse; or when the issues are so complex that the judge simply needs much more information.

A comprehensive evaluation usually lasts between two and six months and is very expensive, sometimes costing up to $10,000. The evaluations are conducted by a psychologist or psychologist that has been qualified and approved and can be found on the Maricopa county court roster. On the roster you will find providers locations, prices and credentials.

Comprehensive assessments usually include mental health testing for both parties. It may also include diagnoses. There is typically an in-depth analysis of all allegations made.

The results of these assessments are provided to the parties, attorneys if they have them, and to judges. They can be between 20 and 60 pages. One interesting thing to note, is that the recommendation in the evaluation may not be legally sound, since the providers are not typically attorneys. If you received the results of an evaluation and you think they are wrong, consider consulting with an attorney in order to find out the legal basis for the recommendations.

Limited Family Assessment

A limited family assessment is similar to the comprehensive one, just more limited nature. This is more appropriate when there are fewer issues and a host of mental testing is not necessary or warranted. These evaluations are typically focused on specific issues like where a gifted child should attend school or whether a parent should be allowed to move away with the child. They cost less than the comprehensive family assessment and take less time to complete.

Therapeutic Intervention

Therapeutic interventions are appropriate when there is a pressing crisis within the family. Emergency case stabilization might be ordered to add an emergency hearing before temporary orders are issued. A typical case might be where, amidst the contentious custody case, one or both parents are on drugs, teenagers may be using drugs or failing at school, and there maybe allegations of domestic violence.

The goal of the emergency case stabilization is to get a plan in place to stabilize the children and parents while they get further treatment and more investigation is conducted.

Therapeutic Reunification

Therapeutic reunification therapy is typically ordered when one parent has been missing for a long time or estrangement between the parent and child has happened for other reasons. The purpose is for the therapist to assist the parent and the child in re-establishing a relationship.

This would also be appropriate in cases where the relationship is severely damaged for other reasons. If the parent has exposed the child to domestic violence, sub- stance abuse, child abuse or neglect then it is possible you would need reunification therapy even without a prolonged absence of one parent.

Parenting Coordinator

A parenting coordinator (PC) is a court appointed third party who is given quasi-judicial authority and remains involved after the court has entered either an initial order or a modification/order of contempt on your current case. Maricopa County has a roster of different available parenting coordinators. If you check out the list, you will see that there are a wide variety of backgrounds, training and styles that a parenting coordinator may have.

The statutes allow for the appointment of a Parenting Coordinator if:

1. the parents are persistently in conflict with one another;
2. there is a history of substance abuse by either parent or family violence;
3. there are serious concerns about the mental health or behavior of either parent;
4. a child has special needs; or
5. it would otherwise be in the children's best interests to do so.

In order to get on the list, a person must be a psychiatrist, psychologist, behavioral therapist, nurse or nurse practitioner or an attorney. In addition to the licensure required above they must have received at least six hours of both domestic violence and child abuse training and receive ongoing training in these areas. Additionally, each PC must receive additional forensic training on issues like child development, alienation of children, relocation issues, high conflict families, impact of high conflict on children, adults, and families, report writing, family court law, cultural diversity, interviewing and assessment skills, role boundaries, informed consent, mandated reporting of abuse, and testimonial issues.

Since each PC brings a unique background, it is important to determine your needs and your particular situation prior to selecting a PC.

How do I get a Parenting Coordinator?

You can request the court appoint a parenting coordinator. You and your ex must stipulate to a specific parenting coordinator or if there are two attorneys on a case, they can work together to select a parenting coordinator who is a good fit for your issues. The Maricopa County Superior court roster will show you where the providers are physically located on a map and how much they cost.

How much do Parenting Coordinators cost and who pays for them?

PCs typically charge anywhere between $200 and $400 per hour and are paid for by the parties either equally or in some proportion to their incomes. While this is expensive, it is usually less expensive and more effective than both people paying attorneys. It is also faster than waiting for a Judge to weigh in on your specific issue.

Notes

Chapter 6
Divorce Negotiations

The goal of a divorce or family law case is always to settle the case. In the vast majority of cases, parties are better able to reach workable agreements than a judge who rules on the issues. You know your issues, your children, your goals and your fears much better than a judge and you are in a better position to get what you want in a negotiation.

Taking the time to think about how to negotiate is therefore in your best interest. This section is to get you thinking about how to tackle the negotiation piece of your divorce or family law case.

Determining what is most important to you is an essential component for preparing to negotiate, as is thinking about what is most important to the other party. It may be possible to meet both of your objectives.

Much has been written about negotiations and this chapter will not replace reading the classic books on the subject like *Getting to Yes* or *Influence*. It will give you some practical and theoretical tips for how to negotiate a favorable outcome in your divorce.

The environment for divorce negotiation

Before you do anything else, first set the environment for your negotiation.

This reminds me of an episode of *Ray Donovan*. It's a Showtime series and Ray Donovan is an L.A. fixer. He works for a law firm and comes in to clean up big messes. He's an expert negotiator and works completely outside the legal system. In one episode, Ray walks into a room where a big 'gangsta' thug is sitting across from the law partner he works for. The gangsta has two more thugs on either side of him and a pistol on the table. The law partner is sitting across the huge man sweating profusely.

The first thing Ray does is kick out the extra thugs "Get them outta here." Then he demands that the gun be removed. Before he begins to address the terms of the negotiation, he sets the environmental stage. So how can we apply this to you?

A Negotiation Between Equals

It can be very difficult in cases where there is a imbalance of power, particularly if one spouse has controlled or abused the other. If there is a large age gap between the parties or a big difference in life experience, education or careers you may have an imbalance of power. **If you do not feel that you can have a negotiation between equals, you will need an advocate.** This could be an attorney or a lay legal advocate. It should *not* be an interested or related party like a new spouse, significant other or parent.

Where to Negotiate

A negotiation should take place in neutral territory. This is different for everyone. For some, the kitchen table may be a fine place for a negotiation. For others, a Starbucks half-way between two homes may work. For this reason, it may be preferable to avoid meeting at one attorney's office. The space should be comfortable for both parties and non-threatening. It doesn't necessarily have to be private. Sometimes a restaurant negotiation can be very effective, especially because the act of eating together can sometimes break the ice. In some cultures, a meal or drink must be shared prior to engaging in any negotiations. It helps to humanize the other party and break down the walls that may have come into the meeting.

When I hold informal settlement conferences in my office, I try to always have pas- tries and drinks available. Setting the stage for comfort and safety is essential in a good negotiation strategy.

Who Should Be Present

Only the relevant players should participate in the negotiation. This comes up frequently in divorce and family law cases. A parent or spouse may want to participate in the negotiation. They want to act as your ally. You may, or may not, want that too. It is almost always a BAD idea. The third party has an agenda and it may not line up with your agenda.

You and your spouse (or the other parent) are the only parties to the case and the decisions should be made by you.

With that being said, having someone looking out for your interests present can be a very good idea.

Decide in Advance of the Procedure

Everyone should know what they are walking into before getting to the meeting. Negotiations can take place in one, long meeting, or in a series of meetings over weeks and months. Before you engage in the negotiation process, you should determine and communicate what the procedure will be for negotiation.

For instance, you may determine that at the first meeting you will identify the relevant issues and initial positions as well as any materials that will need to be gathered prior to the next meeting. You may set a deadline for when those materials must be provided and schedule a follow up meeting where you intend to flush out the materials and see if any agreements can/will be reached. Decide in advance whether you are open to or you expect the other party to sign a binding agreement at the negotiation. Sometimes parties reach agreements, draft them and sign them at a given meeting and other times the parties take their agreements home for consideration, both are valid options.

Ask yourself these questions before deciding on the procedure of your negotiation.

- Are you someone who needs time to process before making decisions?
- Do you ever regret decisions that you have made when buying a car or making another decision without fully contemplating and committing to the consequences?
- Are you someone who thinks quickly on their feet and processes information and decisions quickly?

Think about and decide in advance how you would like the procedure of the negotiation to flow. Make sure this is communicated and agreed upon prior to starting the negotiation. Once people start reaching agreements, no matter how small, it is easier to keep saying yes. Use this to your advantage by starting with easy agreements on procedure before diving into divisive issues.

Emotions and Negotiation

Divorce and family law is emotional. Nothing is more emotional than the things that matter most to you and divorce touches all of them; your relationships, love, children, money, security, stability. Our emotions are always a factor in negotiating your divorce or family law case.

Traditionally, we have been taught to "separate the problem from the people" when negotiating. Not only is this impossible, it ignores the role of emotions and the impact they have on negotiating.

Recently, research has revealed the role that emotions play when we are in the midst of a negotiation. Anxiety is the number one emotion people experience in negotiations, and, it is associated with comparatively worse outcomes. In a recent study, anxious subjects had lower expectations, made lower first offers, responded more quickly to offers, and exited the bargaining sooner. And—no surprise—they got worse outcomes.

We know that positive emotions lead to increased creativity. So the higher your "emotional intelligence," the better outcome you can expect to achieve in negotiations.

Emotionally intelligent people have the capacity to:

- identify the emotions they and others are experiencing;
- understand how those emotions affect their thinking;
- use that knowledge to achieve better outcomes;
- productively manage emotions, tempering or intensifying them for whatever your specific purpose.

What does this mean for you? Preparing emotionally is just as important as preparing for the substance of your negotiation. Music or meditation can be successfully used to help you get into the zone of calm and focused. You want to be calm and keep your anxiety to a minimum while at the same time staying aware of the potential pitfalls in your negotiation.

Legal vs. Practical Leverage

Negotiation does not have to be a zero sum gain. The best settlements result in a win-win. As lawyers, we tend to think in terms of "what the judge might do" or what "the law says." When you are settling your divorce case, there is no judge and there is no law (subject to some limitations). For the most part, you can do whatever works best for you and the other party. Most of the limitations come down to parenting time and child support. A child support worksheet must be filed even if the parties decide to depart from the guidelines. Similarly, a judge must approve any parenting time arrangement as "in the best interest of the child". Practically speaking, agreements between parties are rarely rejected and you are not bound by the law when determining how you wish to divide your property or parent your children.

Legally, many things do not matter. Your affair, his spending problem, and your interfering mother-in-law do not typically have a place in the divorce court action. In Arizona, divorces are no-fault, meaning only facts related to specific elements of the law will be relevant and admissible. That simply isn't the case when engaged in negotiations.

For instance, a soon to be ex-husband was anxious to get remarried to his new girlfriend and the wedding was planned for Hawaii the following month. The trial wasn't to take place for three more months. He was desperate to settle. That gave the wife leverage to negotiate the terms of her divorce. So when preparing for the negotiation, think about everything related to each parties' considerations and motivations. As much as possible, try to get inside the head of the opposing party. This will help you be creative in coming up with proposals and solutions.

Help when negotiating

Unfortunately, when the stakes are highest, we are often at our worst when it comes to communicating. Our creativity shuts down as our panic levels rise. One option to make negotiations easier might be having a third-party intermediary shuttle between the parties.

Mediators

A mediator is a trained neutral third party whose job is to facilitate communication and agreements. They are not there to advise you. They are not supposed to insert their opinions. Mediators are used for all sorts of dispute resolution, not just divorce. When selecting a mediator for your divorce, make sure the person has experience in divorce. A background in psychology can also be very helpful.

A mediator should help you to set the environment, procedures, and help keep emotions in check. Sometimes, a face-to-face negotiation is counter-productive to reaching an agreement and the mediator may separate the parties. This is called a "caucus". The parties are separated into their own rooms and the mediator goes back and forth with different offers. This can help keep the emotion out of the way and generally allows people to reach agreements faster.

There are definite advantages to bringing in a mediator and using shuttle mediation tactics. Reaching settlement is almost always better than litigating, not just for the current outcome but for the future relationships of the parties.

Further, one of the greatest advantages of reaching settlement within your divorce is that it sets the stage for your future negotiations and communications with your soon-to-be ex-spouse. If you and your spouse are only able to communicate through a third-party mediator you are not getting the full advantages of divorce negotiation and settlement. If the two of you have children, you may need to continue communicating for years and avoiding the court room now and in the future should be a mutual goal. If you cannot be in the same room together, this may make future communications more difficult- or expensive- if you need a mediator.

Attorneys

Attorneys can also negotiate on your behalf without the use of a mediator. When both parties are represented, or even if one party is represented, an attorney may help the two of you reach an agreement. An attorney is not a neutral third party. They are an advocate and ally for the client only. They can provide you legal advice and guidance as well as perspective and options. (They can let you know if you are about to enter into a bad agreement, while the mediator cannot).

Culture when negotiating

There is this fun icon based on a Harvard Business Review article on negotiations. It compares and contrasts emotional expression vs. confrontation by region and the results are very interesting.

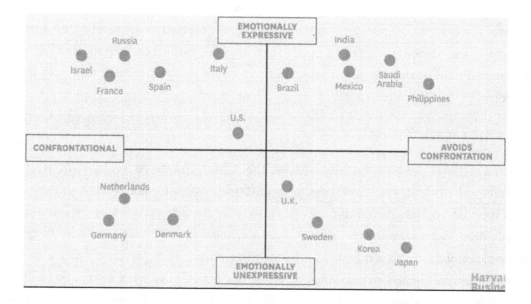

From the image, we can get an idea of how different cultures perceive and receive emotional intensity and confrontation. While you know your spouse better than most, it's a good idea to think about your cultural background surrounding confrontation and emotions and your spouse's cultural background. Thinking about and considering these issues may help you to design a negotiation procedure that will be most helpful to you.

If you have very different styles of negotiation and expression, it may be one more reason to enlist the help of a third party.

Just keep talking or stop!

John Kerry, serving as Secretary of State as of this writing, has recently brokered agreements with Syria during peace talks that have lasted many months. Kerry just wouldn't give up and just kept talking. If you are seriously committed to reaching a settlement, you should not give up! Recognize that coming to an agreement may take many months, but it is almost always worth the effort.

At the same time, sometimes the very best technique is to just stop talking. Let the silence linger. Allow people time to think and respond and surely consider your requests. The desire to reach a settlement and to just keep negotiating should be tempered by the understanding that sometimes these things can take time and multiple sessions.

When to walk away

When you have laid everything out on the table, you have brought in third-party neutrals to help you, you have kept your emotions in check and you have used all the leverage that you have available to you, it may be time to walk away. Sometimes two people don't even seem to be talking about the same case. One parent may be alleging domestic violence and drug use and the other parent may say they had a perfectly normal relationship absent any abuse whatsoever. If you have tried every- thing and you are not in the same universe, it may be time to walk away and head to trial. Check out your original analysis of best case and worst case scenario back when you identified your issues and objectives, and compare it to the offers you have on the table with your negotiation. It should help you evaluate the reasonableness of the negotiation.

Notes

_____

_____

_____

_____

_____

_____

_____

_____

_____

_____

_____

_____

_____

Chapter 7
Trial Preparation and Trial Presentation

Let's quickly review to see what you've accomplished so far: You began preparing for trial as you started this process when you determined your objectives. You continued preparing for trial when you outlined which issues applied to you and when you took the time to identify the evidence (documents and witnesses) that would assist you in proving your case. Now is where the legal analysis gets important.

Most often at this point, you will have already filed your initial paperwork, responded, appeared for a temporary orders hearing and/or an RMC. Additionally, you will have attended a parenting conference or met with some other court-appointed third-party provider, and you would have attended court-ordered Alternative Dispute Resolution (ADR) or mediation. Following the mediation, you probably had a telephonic or in-person status conference with the judge to determine if any agreements had been reached. If you are here, you either did not reach any agreements or you have some, but not all, outstanding issues you intend to lay before a judge.

The best trial preparation begins many months before trial, but most often, a hearing will be set within three months of the status conference. It is time to make strategic decisions, get organized, and execute your strategy.

1. Identify which broad legal issues are remaining.
2. Identify the actual law (from the Arizona Revised Statutes) that applies to the legal issues.
3. Drill down to determine the elements of each legal issue.
4. Identify the facts from your case that apply to each legal element.
5. Identify the evidence to support the facts for each element of each legal issue.
6. Finalize your exhibit and witness lists and disclose any items or witnesses that have not been disclosed.
7. Draft your pretrial statement.

8. Prepare your testimony.
9. Present your case.
10. Review your decree.

We will look at each of these 10 steps in detail as applied to a hypothetical case.

Identify which broad legal issues are remaining.

Suppose you started off with a divorce case with issues that included property division, child support, spousal maintenance, custody, attorney's fees, valuing a business, separate property, and hidden money or waste. By applying our negotiation tactics and attending the court-ordered ADR, you have settled all of the issues except spousal maintenance.

In our example case, you will need to prepare to litigate the issue of spousal maintenance.

Identify the actual law (from the Arizona Revised Statutes) that applies to the legal issue.

With the only remaining issue identified as spousal maintenance, you go to the Arizona Revised Statutes (or the chapter on spousal maintenance) to determine the specific language of the law, A.R.S. 25-319 (do look to the law because it is possible that the language or factors may have changed since the release of this book).

Drill down to determine the elements of each legal issue.

To establish a legally binding contract, a person must show there was a valid offer, acceptance of that offer, and consideration that was paid for the contact. The offer, acceptance and consideration are the three elements that must be proven. Likewise, in family law, each law has factors, elements or considerations that make up the law. For each issue, we must identify the corresponding elements.

We know based on the language of the law that spousal maintenance is a two-step analysis and that the person seeking maintenance must qualify (and has the bur- den of showing they qualify) before the court will apply step two to determine the amount and duration of maintenance.

The spouse seeking maintenance must show he or she qualifies by documenting any one of the following:

- Property, including property received in the divorce, is insufficient to provide for his or her reasonable needs;
- The spouse is unable to be self-sufficient through appropriate work, or lacks enough earning ability in the labor market to be self-sufficient, or takes care of a child whose age or condition requires the spouse to not work outside the home;
- The spouse contributed to the educational or career opportunities of the other spouse; or
- The marriage was for long duration and the spouse is of an age that prevents them from employment adequate to be self-sufficient.

Once the court finds the spouse seeking maintenance has established one or more of the above qualifiers, the court must consider the following factors in order to decide how much spousal maintenance to award, and how long it should last.

From the language of the statute, we know that the court will consider:

1. Standard of living established during the marriage.
2. Duration of the marriage.
3. Age, employment history, earning ability, and physical and emotional condition of the spouse seeking maintenance.
4. Ability of the spouse requested to pay to meet his or her own needs while paying maintenance.
5. Comparative financial resources of the spouses, including their comparative earning abilities in the labor market.
6. Contribution of the spouse seeking maintenance to the earning ability of the other spouse.
7. Extent to which the maintenance-seeking spouse reduced his or her income or career opportunities for the benefit of the other spouse.
8. Ability of both parties after the dissolution to contribute to the future educational costs of their mutual children.

9. Financial resources of the party seeking maintenance, including marital property awarded in the divorce, and that spouse's ability to meet his or her own needs independently.

10. Time necessary to acquire sufficient education or training so that the maintenance-seeking spouse may find appropriate employment, and whether such education or training is readily available.

11. Excessive or abnormal expenditures, destruction, concealment or fraudulent disposition of community, joint tenancy and other property held in common.

12. Cost for the maintenance-seeking spouse to obtain health insurance and the reduction in the cost of health insurance for the spouse from whom maintenance is sought, if the latter is able to convert family health insurance to employee health insurance after the marriage is dissolved.

13. All actual damages and judgments from conduct that results in criminal conviction of either spouse in which the other spouse or child was the victim.

Identify the facts from your case that applies to each legal element

This can be one of the hardest steps for people who are representing themselves. You are being asked to look at your whole life, everything that has ever happened, all the complexities of you and your family and determine "the facts" relevant to the elements!

In our hypothetical case the relevant facts are:

Husband and Wife are both in their early fifties. Husband works as an engineer for Intel. Wife worked minimally throughout the 30-year marriage and raised the parties' three children. She has a bachelor's degree with very little work experience. The parties' total community value is just under $1 million, which includes a house and retirement funds.

- Property, including property received in the divorce, is insufficient to provide for his or her reasonable needs;
- the spouse is unable to be self-sufficient through appropriate work, or lacks enough earning ability in the labor market to be self-sufficient, or takes care of a child whose age or condition requires the spouse to not work outside the home;
- the spouse contributed to the educational or career opportunities of the other spouse; or

- the marriage was for long duration and the spouse is of an age that prevents them from employment adequate to be self-sufficient.

A legal analysis and application of facts looks like this:

Based on these facts, Wife has insufficient property to provide for her needs, b cause after she receives her portion of the community property, there will not be sufficient income from that property to support her. The asset value of the home and retirement funds are tied up until either the sale of the home or her retirement. Even then, it will be insufficient to provide for her on a long-term basis.

Further, Wife is unable to be self-sufficient under factor two because she is not employed full-time and has only worked minimally throughout the marriage for the last 30 years. She cannot immediately enter the labor market and command employment that would allow her to be self-sufficient.

Additionally, Wife supported Husband's career by taking the majority of the child-rearing duties and maintaining the household while Husband traveled, worked late and enjoyed the flexibility in his career that he would not have had if Wife wasn't taking care of the home and children.

Under factor four, Wife has been married for more than 30 years, so the parties have a marriage of long duration. Whether she is of an age that precludes her from becoming self-sufficient isn't clear.

In this case, Wife qualifies for spousal maintenance under factors one, two, three and possibly four. The court should then analyze step 2 to determine the amount and duration of maintenance.

Identify the evidence to support the facts for each element of each legal issue

Wife must prove:

- Age
- duration of marriage

- her work history
- Husband's work history
- How Wife supported Husband's career
- total value of the community property and the nature of the property
- future earning capacity

Wife's testimony will establish most of the relevant facts, and many will not be in dispute; the couple already established the nature and value of the property via settlement. Wife may also want to show a résumé with her complete work history and she may want to hire an expert witness to testify as to her future earning capacity. She may have a journal or calendar she wants to use to show how she supported her husband's career. Under this step, Wife should list the items and witnesses she will use to prove she qualifies for maintenance. Husband should gather any contrary evidence. For instance, if Wife worked minimally during the marriage as a physician, he will want to produce evidence of available positions for physicians, her license, and what she could earn as a physician.

The same analysis should be done for the second set of spousal maintenance factors to determine amount and duration.

Finalize your exhibit and witness lists and disclose any items or witnesses that have not been disclosed

Make a list of each item and each witness that you may call. It is better to disclose any item or witness that you don't think you will need than to be prevented from calling the witness or introducing the evidence at a later time. Look back at your disclosure statements to ensure everything and everyone has been disclosed.

Draft your pretrial statement

Your pretrial statement is the most important document in your entire case. The pretrial statement contains all of the jurisdictional information, all of the uncontested facts of the case, the procedural history, outstanding issues, positions and legal analysis. Most judges prefer a joint pretrial statement, which means your positions and legal analysis is listed in the same document as your spouse's. The pretrial will contain a list of exhibits, witnesses, objections to the opposing party's exhibits or witnesses, and an inventory of your property and debts.

Follow a template to draft your pretrial statement using Access Legal or another form or template for the county you are in. If you can get the assistance of an attorney with only one item, let this be the item. Many times, a judge forms their decision based on this document prior to you ever setting foot in the courtroom.

You will also use the pretrial statement as your outline for trial presentation. You already listed out the relevant facts to each element; in trial, you will need a witness or exhibit to testify as to each relevant fact in order to support your claims.

Prepare your testimony

Once the pretrial statement is drafted and filed with the court, you can now prepare your testimony and the testimony of any other witnesses you are calling. Use the pretrial statement as a guide for the facts you need to get into evidence and design your questions to elicit the response you want.

Practice telling your story, with all of the relevant facts, in a calm and clear manner.

You want your pretrial to tell a story and present both a legal and factual theory consistent with that story. If you can, find someone who has a legal background and who is relatively unfamiliar with the case. Go through your testimony and then ask them what they thought or if they were unclear about any particular statements you made.

You must also prepare yourself to be cross-examined and to cross-examine the opposing party and other witnesses. More on that next.

Present your case

On the day of your court case, you will be nervous. Try to get a good night's sleep beforehand. Eat good food and don't go into court hyped up on caffeine. Some people take anti-anxiety medicine before going to court and swear it helps. Just don't try it for the first time on the day of your hearing. You don't want to risk being drowsy in front of the judge.

In family court, opening statements are not typically presented and the pretrial statement takes the place of your opening statement. The Petitioner will present his or her case first.

First, you will be sworn in. If you do not have an attorney, you may testify from the counsel table or you may come to the witness box. Then you will offer statements of fact that support your legal positions. One of the biggest mistakes people make is testifying as to their feelings, conclusions or assumptions. You will want to practice before court as to how you will convey to the judge the FACTS that support your conclusions.

For instance, you want to testify that "He is such a bad father." This will not go over well at all. You may think this is a fact, but it is your opinion; your statements must be based on facts. Instead, you should say: "He drinks alcohol on a daily basis and fails to feed the children dinner. Father calls me each evening drunk with slurred words after having admitted to drinking 12 beers. He doesn't supervise homework and the children are late to school when with Father. Exhibit 2 shows the children's tardy records and you will see that on Tuesday-Thursday, when the children are with Father, they are tardy 75% of the time. Additionally, the child care records, marked as exhibit 4, show that Father checks the children in at 6:30 a.m. and picks them up after 6:00 p.m. 85% of the time that he has the children."

Do you see the difference? The other thing you can do to help the judge is to state before you testify which issue and element you will be addressing. For instance, you can say:

"Your honor, I want to offer testimony on what is in the best interest of the child, specifically with regards to Mother's mental health. Mother has struggled with mental illness for the last 10 years. Exhibit 12 shows her mental health records and that she was diagnosed with agoraphobia. She has extreme levels of anxiety, doesn't drive or have a license, and won't leave the house for days at a time. Her mental health status affects the best interest of our daughter because Mom is unable to take her to school, doctors appointments, or extracurricular activities due to her mental illness."

When referencing exhibits, you have two options. You can agree in advance (stipulate) which exhibits will be admitted. This is the simplest, fastest way to use exhibits. This requires that you and the opposing party agree in advance not to object to exhibits. Keep in mind that the only valid objections to exhibits are that they are not relevant, they were not disclosed, they are prejudicial to the point where the prejudice outweighs the value of the exhibit, or they are duplicative. The second way to get an exhibit admitted is to "offer to admit" the exhibit. The opposing party has the opportunity to object based on the objections laid out above. If you do not offer to admit the exhibits, the judge cannot look at your exhibit.

Offer your testimony in a detailed, specific and organized fashion, walking the judge through the issues you are addressing one at a time. When you are done testifying, the opposing party will have the opportunity to cross-examine you.

When conducting cross-examination, the general rule is that you should not ask a question of the witness when you do not know the answer. A good cross-examination asks leading questions where you are actually doing most of the examination. A good cross might be something like this:

"Father, isn't it true that when Mother receives treatment for agoraphobia her symptoms disappear completely? And isn't it true that in the 10 years you have been married you have left the state on business trips approximately 30% of the time? Isn't it true that during that time Mother has always gotten the children to school and doctors visits? I'm showing you what has been marked as exhibit 15. Can you identify exhibit 15? These are medical records of your daughter showing Mother took your daughter to the doctor, correct? And isn't it true that maternal grandmother lives with Mother and provides any and all of the necessary transportation?"

After cross-examination, the moving party (party offering evidence) can "redirect." That means you may offer testimony or ask questions regarding anything brought up during cross-examination. After redirect, you can call any other witnesses and proceed in the same fashion. The judge may interject and ask questions too. After the Petitioner has "rested" their case, the Respondent has the same opportunity to present evidence.

Judges keep a close eye on the clock to make sure that each party uses only half of the time allotted for trial. We almost always run out of time and wish we had more time to present our evidence. We also always feel discombobulated. We plan for an organized and perfect presentation of evidence, but it never goes as planned. The better prepared you are, the better you will feel, but plan to be flexible. There are almost always surprises.

At the end of your allotted trial time, the judge will most likely take the matter "under advisement." This means he or she will not issue a ruling. You will not be divorced. This can be hugely disappointing, but the judge needs the time to examine the exhibits and draft a ruling. You should receive the ruling within 60 days.

Review your decree

When you get the ruling, the new time clock starts ticking. You have a finite amount of time to request a motion for reconsideration, to request a new trial, or to file a notice of appeal. If there is a problem with your ruling, get help from an attorney quickly. At Modern Law we have a post-decree meeting where we discuss these options in depth because important decisions need to be made.

After the hearing, keep in mind what is modifiable and what is non-modifiable as well as the timeframe for each issue you are interested in modifying.

Courtroom Etiquette

Courtrooms are some of the most formal environments in our society today, more formal than most churches or fine dining restaurants. Judges expect that you will know and understand courtroom etiquette, but rarely are people given instructions on what is expected.

1. Be on time.
2. You need to be dressed formally and appropriately.
   a. Pants or skirts that are no shorter than 2 inches above the knee (no shorts)
   b. Collared shirts for men – no T-shirts
   c. No blue jeans – or your very best pair of jeans if you cannot find slacks – no holes
   d. For women – no cleavage
3. Stand up when the judge enters the courtroom and sit down only after they have done so.

4. Be polite to the staff, bailiff, opposing parties, and others in the courtroom.

5. Speak more formally than you might otherwise be inclined to do. For instance, instead of saying "yeah" or "uh-huh" say "Yes, Judge."

6. Treat the judge with flawless deference.

   a. Address the judge only when the judge invites you to do so

   b. Always refer to the judge as "Judge" or "Your Honor"

   c. Do not sneer, scoff, argue or make rude comments to the judge

7. Hide your disdain for the opposing party. Do not interrupt the opposing party or the judge or witnesses on the stand.

Notes

PART III

Chapter 8

Divorce in Arizona

Many people feel overwhelmed, scared, regretful, or guilty when they think about divorce. The legal process seems cloaked in secrecy and the filing clerks sure aren't helping. If you have to hear they can't give you "legal advice" one more time, you may lose your cool.

You are reaching out for information and it seems like it is either not available or there is simply too much to process. You have friends telling you conflicting stories about what you can expect in terms of child support, alimony or spousal maintenance, and who will keep the house.

Have no fear! Modern Law provides step-by-step email instructions on the Arizona Divorce Process, free webinars on all aspects of Arizona Divorce, and an entire Do- it-yourself Divorce website too. This chapter will walk you through the basic aspects of divorce in Arizona.

No-Fault Divorce

Arizona is a no-fault divorce state. This means that unless you have entered into a covenant marriage, anyone can get divorced if they want to do so. Even if your spouse "won't agree." By following the Arizona divorce laws, you will be ensured a divorce regardless of whether or not your spouse will agree to your terms.

Legal Separation vs. Divorce

Many clients ask if a legal separation is a good option for them. If you are considering a legal separation, it is important to understand the legal consequences, as well as the benefits and risks of an Arizona legal separation vs. an Arizona divorce.

The procedure for obtaining a legal separation is the same as a divorce, and will be discussed below. Legally, all of the same rules and laws apply, except at the end of the day, you are not free to remarry.

In both a legal separation and divorce, the court will distribute final orders that stipulate division of spousal assets and debts, legal decision-making and parenting time determinations, and details regarding spousal support and/or child support. The marital community will be severed when the Petition for Legal Separation is served upon the other spouse.

In both legal separation and divorce, the obligations and rights between the two spouses are terminated under Arizona community property law. However, legal separation does not restore the right of either spouse to remarry. Of course in divorce, each spouse walks away "single" and is free to remarry if he or she wishes.

Although orders will be given by the court in both situations, there are some reasons why a legal separation may be preferable to a divorce. For example, a couple may not actually be sure they want to end the marriage. Some couples try legal separation as a "trial" to see whether they wish to terminate the marriage or attempt to work things out. Other issues may exist, like concern over continuous healthcare coverage, or religious beliefs regarding divorce.

Some couples recognize the cost a divorce or dissolution would result in to one party. If a spouse has significant health issues and the cost of health insurance would be prohibitive, the parties may choose to pursue a legal separation in order that the spouse needing the medical insurance may remain on the other spouse's coverage. There are a myriad of other reasons a couple may decide on legal separation instead of divorce. Most importantly, such a decision should be that of the couple—what suits their needs best?

While many people who become legally separated ultimately dissolve their marriage, this is certainly not true for everyone. Arizona law states that in a legal separation, the marital community is severed and any property acquired by a spouse after serving a petition for dissolution, legal separation, or annulment, is the separate property of that spouse—**IF** the petition results in a decree, whether of dissolution, legal separation, or annulment.

In addition to the court entering final orders in either a divorce or a legal separation, the parties may enter into an agreement that's specific to their needs and wishes, and submit it to the court. The court will usually find the agreements binding. How- ever, after considering the terms of the legal separation agreement, and considering the economic circumstances of the parties and other relevant evidence, the court may find the agreement unfair, for support, custody, and parenting time of children. In that case, even if the parties agree, the court could enter an order rejecting the parties' agreement.

Uncontested Divorce

How to Get an Uncontested Divorce in Arizona

There is no specific process for filing an uncontested divorce. Unlike many other states, Arizona does not have a fast-track process for uncontested divorce.

Even when you and your spouse agree on everything when facing a divorce, the pro- cess can still be fairly daunting and complicated. There are several options for how to move forward and a few key things that need to take place.

One spouse must file a petition for dissolution. This is how all divorces start, regard- less of whether or not the spouses agree on the terms. The filing spouse will become the Petitioner and the responding spouse the Respondent. The petition can be general or specific. If the petition is very specific and includes all of the terms agreed upon by both spouses, then you may be able to move forward via default.

After the petition is filed, it must be served upon the opposing party, the other spouse. Service can take place in one of many ways, including personal service or by having the responding spouse sign an acceptance of service. Within 20 days of being served, the responding spouse may file an answer or allow the time to lapse and proceed via default.

To proceed via default, the answering spouse will do nothing. The petitioning spouse can file an application of default after the 20 days has elapsed and then 10 days later ask the judge to sign an order of default. At that point, the terms of the petition will control the divorce.

There are a few things to watch out for if proceeding by default. You must make sure to address all issues in the Petition. I recommend including a **detailed property settlement agreement and parenting plan** that you attach and incorporate in your petition.

Another sticky area is that there is a 60-day mandatory waiting period from the time you file the petition until you can legally become divorced. We usually wait until 60 days have passed after you have served the petition before you file the application of default.

The other option for moving forward when you both agree to all terms of your divorce is by *consent decree*. Here, one spouse files the petition, serves the other party and the served party files a response. Sixty days later, the two spouses file a signed consent decree. In some ways, this is a cleaner, easier way to get divorced.

If you move forward by default and you have minor children, it is possible the judge may not accept the terms in the petition. On the other hand, if you proceed with a consent decree, it is crystal clear that you both intended the terms you signed off on and it is very unlikely that one spouse will be able to change their mind later.

Default judgments can be set aside, so by choosing the default option you may be leaving the door open to having the other party try to contest the judgment later. On the plus side, if you move forward via default, only one filing fee must be paid, the fee for the petition. The respondent never files a response and therefore escapes the fee.

Arizona Divorce Law

In the event that you and your spouse do not agree on some or all issues in your divorce, Arizona divorce laws will determine the outcome for any unresolved issues. If you and your spouse agree to work outside the Arizona divorce laws, you can determine your own fate. With very few exceptions, the court will accept whatever agreements you and your spouse reach on the following issues.

- Property division
- Debt division

- Alimony or spousal maintenance
- Child support
- Child custody legal decision-making
- Parenting time
- Attorney fees

Property and Debt Division

Arizona is a community property state. When you married, you and your spouse formed a partnership, called the community. Arizona laws consider everything that happened after you married to be for the benefit of the community. There is a strong presumption that all property and debts be divided equally when you get divorced. There are exceptions, of course. Any money that has been inherited or was gifted to you will be separate property and not subject to division by the court. It is important not to co-mingle separate assets with community assets, or a judge may determine that all of the property will be considered community property. Learn more on community property in chapter   .

Child Custody and Parenting Time

If you are getting a divorce in Arizona and have children, you will need to file a "petition for dissolution of a non-covenant marriage with children" to begin the process. In addition to the property and monetary issues, you will also need to address custody, parenting time, and child support.

Arizona strongly prefers joint custody, now called joint legal decision-making. Un- less one parent is unfit, the court is very likely to order that parents share joint legal decision-making. Joint legal decision-making means that both parents must work together to make decisions regarding:

- Medical care and treatment,
- Religious decisions,
- Educational decisions, and
- Personal care decisions for the child.

Parenting time will be ordered based on the best interest of the child, but the court will assume that equal parenting time, when possible, is in the best interest of the child. Special rules apply in situations involving domestic violence and substance abuse.

Arizona child support. Child support in Arizona, and all states, is pursuant to a calculator. Inputs into the calculator include both parent's income (not including their spouse's or roommates' income), health insurance expenses, other children, spousal maintenance paid and received, extraordinary expenses, and parenting time. Unless otherwise agreed by the parents, the court almost always orders the presumed guidelines child support. Learn more on child support in chapter .

Spousal Maintenance or Alimony. What is referred to as alimony in most states is called spousal maintenance in Arizona. Unlike child support, there is no calculator to determine the amount or duration of spousal maintenance. However, we have developed a spousal maintenance estimator you can find on our website, www.mymodernlaw.com.

Relocation. Because Arizona favors joint legal decision-making and equal parenting time, relocation of one parent with the children is very difficult. The burden is on the moving parent to show the move is in the best interest of the child and how the moving parent will minimize the impact on the relationship between the children and the non-moving parent.

Arizona Divorce Process

Every Arizona divorce case begins with the filing Petition in Family Court. The first step in the Arizona divorce process will either be filing the petition or responding to the petition, so the first thing we will tackle are these initial filings in Family Court.

Arizona Family Court

In Maricopa County, all family court cases are heard "in family court." This means there are assigned judges who only hear family law cases. They abide by their own local rules and the Arizona Family Law Rules of Civil Procedure. Family court judges are routinely working to improve the process and encourage settlement.

Each Arizona family court case begins with the filing of these initial documents, including the Petition and Response. Either party may or may not also request temporary orders by filing a motion along with the Petition or Response. A temporary order is an order issued during the pendency of a case before a final order is issued. The order could be for child support, maintenance, payment of bills, use of the home or any other matter.

After the initial filings, the next step for the divorce in Arizona is discovery and disclosure, which represents the "meat and potatoes" of your divorce and the beginning of pretrial conferences.

For our clients, this is our next major milestone meeting after the initial consultation or hire date. This meeting is usually in-office and can last up to two hours. During this meeting, we work on getting into the nitty-gritty of your case. We will go over all relevant documents and materials that we will need for your case, both from you and the opposing party. We will go through the Rule 49 disclosure chart and the mandatory disclosures required under Rule 49.

There is some homework before our meeting. Fortunately, we have broken it down into a three-step process to make it easier to handle.

Disclosure and discovery become both negotiation and trial tools. It includes completing your Affidavit of Financial Information. Our system provides you with the tools you need in order to systematically identify and organize all of the evidence you will need for your divorce in Arizona.

Disclosure and Discovery Tools Include:

- Interrogatories
- Request for Production of Documents
- Request for Admissions
- Depositions
- Subpoenas

Pre-Hearing Conferences

When you file for divorce in Arizona, there are a number of non- evidentiary, pre-hearing conferences prior to your final hearing. Non-evidentiary means that wit- nesses and evidence will not be introduced. The judge will make procedural decisions but not substantive decisions. That means that the judge may decide to send you to mediation or when to set a status conference, but the judge will not decide how much your child support will be.

These non-evidentiary pre-hearing conferences may be called any of the following names:

BILLIE TARASCIO BUSTS THESE DIVORCE MYTHS

7 BIG FAT
Child Support Myths
in Arizona

1. MY EX GOT MARRIED AND HAS WAY MORE HOUSEHOLD INCOME NOW. I SHOULD PAY LESS IN CHILD SUPPORT.

Sorry. Your Ex's new spouse has ZERO legal obligation to support your munchkins. His or her income doesn't change how much you owe your ex.

2. WE HAVE EQUAL PARENTING TIME, SO NEITHER PAYS ANY CHILD SUPPORT.

Child support uses parenting time as ONE factor. Other factors include each parent's income, child care costs, insurance costs, and others. Just because you have equal parenting time, does not necessarily mean you don't owe any support.

3. I'VE LOST MY JOB, BUT I JUST CHANGED MY CHILD SUPPORT PAYMENT. I CAN'T ASK FOR A MODIFICATION FOR A YEAR!

When modifying parenting time or legal decision making, you have to wait one year after an order is entered before asking for a modification (absent an emergency). **This is not the case for child support issues**. If changes have occurred that would create more than a 15% change to the actual child support obligation you may ask the court for a modification.

4. I'M GOING TO PRISON AND CAN'T WORK. MY CHILD SUPPORT OBLIGATION WILL BE SUSPENDED.

NO!!!!!!! You must ask for a modification of your child support obligation. So many people get out of prison owing tens of thousands of dollars for unpaid child support. **You must modify a court order to reduce or suspend your obligation.**

5. MY EX AGREED TO MODIFY MY SUPPORT. WE DON'T NEED TO FILE WITH THE COURT.

If there is a court order in place, you mutually agree to change support without facing the possibility of the Court ignoring your agreement. File a stipulated modification changing the child support obligation. Yes, it costs some money now, but will save you thousands later.

6. YOU CAN NEVER GET MORE SUPPORT THAN WHAT THE CHILD SUPPORT CALCULATOR STATES.

In certain cases, you may be eligible for a deviation from the child support guidelines. If, for instance, you child has special needs including tutoring and behavioral support, you may be eligible for a bump up. Similarly, if the child has an independent source of income like a trust fund or money from work as a child actor, you may be able to bump down.

7. MY EX AGREED TO A CHILD SUPPORT AMOUNT, SO THE JUDGE HAS TO ACCEPT IT.

The Judge DOES NOT have to accept an amount that you and your ex agree to for child support. The judge must find that the amount you agreed to is in the best interest of the child. Further, if any of the parents are receiving or have received state assistance, you may have a IV-D case. That means that the State is a party to your case. The State will want to recoup the money paid out in food stamps on behalf of your children by the other parent. In these cases you will need to include the state as a party and serve them with a copy of anything and everything filed in your case.

MODERN LAW

- Resolution Management Conference
- Early Resolution Conference
- Status Conference
- Return Hearing

Note: A Temporary Orders Hearing is an evidentiary hearing. Evidence will be taken and the judge will make decisions regarding substantive legal issues.

Negotiations

For your divorce in Arizona, you will usually be required to engage in some sort of formal negotiation process. This may be mediation through conciliation services (at the courthouse) or an Alternative Dispute Resolution with a Judge Pro Tem. The following are different possibilities for formal and information negotiations processes.

- Alternative Dispute Resolution
- Mediation through Conciliation Services
- Private Mediation
- Settlement Conferences with Lawyers
- Informal negotiations between the parties

Trial Preparation and Trial

It is important to note that most people do not reach this step. Approximately 90% of cases can be settled by diligently going through the process above. With that being said, the last step in the process is preparing your evidence and witnesses for trial and drafting a pretrial statement. Your pretrial statement is the most important document in the trial prep and trial process. If you hire an attorney for only one step in your entire case, this should be the time.

If you find at any point in time you need assistance with your divorce in Arizona, call us, register for a webinar, or email us! We want to hear your story and help come up with a plan!

Notes

Chapter 9
Child Custody

Jim and Monica have three children, Sarah, Katie and Josh. Monica has been a stay at home parent, and Jim has worked in sales throughout the duration of their marriage. Now, Monica wants a divorce and wants to keep the kids full time with Jim paying spousal maintenance. She would like to continue caring for the children full time and have a part time job while they are in school. Jim wants joint custody. See how the law applies to them.

In 2013... the Arizona legislature changed the term child custody or legal custody to "legal decision making", the terms will be used interchangeably within this article. Parenting time now replaces the term "visitation" for parents. All parents have "parenting time" regardless if they are the "custodial parent"

The legislature also removed the term "custodial" parent. The idea is that one parent should not be undermined by being given "visitation" or being deemed the "non-custodial parent". Times have changed and many parents do not live in the same household. A parent should not lose their status simply because they do not live under the same roof.

Sometimes a parent actually becomes more involved after a divorce or the parents have split up, because each parent must develop their own routine. In a marriage, it is easy to divide duties between the spouses. One often takes the primary role for the children, whether that be for morning routine, baths, homework, doctors appointments, etc. When parents split up, this changes.

This is certainly the case with Jim and Monica. While they lived in the same house- hold Monica did the vast majority of the parenting, and Jim felt undermined when- ever he tried to parent. His attempts to set boundaries and routine with his children were thwarted by Monica who felt he was being too strict. Jim was simply trying to instill routine, responsibility and discipline for his children. If the court only looked to who was doing the majority of the parenting while married, Jim would be forever doomed to be a second-class parent. He hopes that the divorce will allow him to become a bigger part of children's lives and teach them values that he and Monica no longer share.

Jurisdiction (UCCJEA)

A state must have jurisdiction over all the parties and the children in order to make any orders affecting them. The Uniform Child Custody Jurisdiction and Enforcement Act (UCCJEA) is a law that has been adopted by 45 states including Arizona in order to make sure that only one state has jurisdiction over a minor child at any given time to avoid "forum shopping" and competing orders.

Forum shopping is the concept that a person may take their children to a state most favorable to their particular position. For instance, in Oregon, courts will only award joint custody if both parents agree. In the event they do not agree, one parent will be given sole custody. In Arizona, there is a strong presumption to award joint custody, even if both parents are seeking sole custody.

In our hypothetical case, Monica may choose to move the children to Oregon, wait for the appropriate residential time frame and then file for divorce there, seeking sole custody. Poor Jim would be hosed as Monica would most likely be granted sole custody. But the UC CJ EA prevents that from happening.

The general rule is that the children's home state is the state where they have resided for the last six months. Each and every petition for divorce or for custody must contain provisions about where the children have lived for the last six months in order to determine the state has proper jurisdiction. If the court lacks jurisdiction, any order is void.

There are several other ways that Arizona could become the home state. There are also emergency jurisdictional provisions built into the UCCJEA:

1. Arizona is the home state of the child on the date of the commencement of the proceeding, or was the home state of the child within six months before the commencement of the proceeding and the child is absent from Arizona but a parent or person acting as a parent continues to live in Arizona; or

2. A court of another state does not have jurisdiction, or a court of the home state of the child has declined to exercise jurisdiction on the grounds that Arizona is the more appropriate forum under A.R.S. §§ 25-1037 or 25-1038 and both of the following are true:

   a. The child and the child's parents, or the child and at least one parent or a person acting as a parent, have a significant connection with Arizona other than mere physical presence, and

   b. Substantial evidence is available in Arizona concerning the child's care, protection, training and personal relationships; or

3. All courts having jurisdiction have declined to exercise jurisdiction on the ground that an Arizona court is the more appropriate forum to determine the custody of the child under A.R.S. §§ 25-1037 or 25-1038; or

4. A court of any other state would not have jurisdiction under the criteria specified in the above provisions.

The UCCJEA can be tricky, if there are special circumstances you will definitely want to consult with a lawyer who can analyze the situation for you and determine if Arizona has jurisdiction.

In the event that two states are fighting over jurisdiction, or both parents have filed in different states, a specific hearing will be held to determine which state is the more proper forum for jurisdiction. The judges from both jurisdictions will get on the phone and the attorneys and parties will be able to present a case for why their particular jurisdiction is the proper forum, most convenient forum, or if some other exception applies.

Legal decision-making (legal custody)

There is much confusion over the actual meaning of legal decision-making or legal custody. That may be why the Arizona Legislature changed the term to legal decision-making, which is arguably a more accurate description of the rights involved. Arizona supports parents who reach legal decision making (custody) and parenting time (visitation) agreements "without the intervention of the courts," and do every- thing In their power to facilitate an agreement. This includes sending parents to parenting conferences, mediation, and court ordered Alternative dispute resolution "ADR".

When parents share joint legal decision making, both parents have equal rights and responsibilities, and neither parent has superior rights. The court assumes that parents will agree about major life decisions such as:

- Education;
- Personal Care;
- Schooling; and
- Health Care;

Anything outside of the major decisions does not fall under the term legal decision-making. Instead, each parent during their parenting time has a wide berth to make decisions about what happens with their children and their day-to-day activities.

The law presumes that divorcing parents will work as a team to raise their children. If either parent feels the joint legal decision making is not in the children's best interests, they can petition the court to have the status of legal decision making changed to sole legal decision making.

Sole Legal Decision Making

Like many jurisdictions, Arizona tends to favor joint legal decision making over sole legal decision making. Before 1979, it was a statutory preference to get custody to the mother of young children. That preference has been abolished and the court is now strictly forbidden from making a custody determination due to gender alone. Sole legal decision making means one parent is granted the custody of the children as well as the power to make decisions for their benefit. It does not mean that the other parent loses all parental rights—they still are entitled to parenting time. A typical situation involving legal decision making could be where the court has found evidence of domestic violence or recent drug or alcohol convictions. When the court has found that evidence that significant domestic violence has occurred. The evidence of that domestic violence is considered contrary to the best interest of the child. The court must then make arrangements for parenting time that protect both the child and the victim. Most often in those cases, the courts may award sole decision making to the victimized parent, with supervised visits for the other parent.

In the event that a parent has been convicted of a drug or alcohol offense in the last 12 months there is a presumption that awarding either joint or sole legal decision-making to that parent is not in the child's best interest.

Parenting Time

Most jurisdictions refer to visitation-the time the non-custodial parent spends with their children. When the children are with one parent, that parent has the right to make any routine decisions for the children, but must provide food, clothing and shelter. Parenting time comes with both rights and responsibilities. Transportation expenses for parenting time can be set by agreement.

Let's look at the actual language of the law:

The court **shall** adopt a parenting plan that provides for both parents to *share legal decision-making regarding their child* and that maximizes their respective parenting time. The court shall not prefer a parent's proposed plan because of the parent's or child's gender.

Courts in Arizona are overwhelmingly ordering joint legal decision making. For example, just this month Joint Legal Decision-Making was ordered when one parent was in jail. In that case, the Judge gave one parent the final decision-making authority.

When creating your parenting plan the primary question is what is in the best interest of the children.

Absent a finding after a hearing that parenting time would endanger the child's physical, mention, moral or emotional health, both parents are entitled to reason- able parenting time to ensure the child has frequent, meaningful, substantial, and continuing contact with both parents.

What is the best interest of the child?

The court will determine legal decision-making and parenting time in accordance with the best interests of the child, and will consider all factors that are relevant to the child's physical and emotional well-being, including:

1. The past, present and potential future relationship between the parent and the child.
2. The interaction and interrelationship of the child with the child's parent or parents, the child's siblings and any other person who may significantly affect the child's best interest.
3. The child's adjustment to home, school and community.
4. If the child is of suitable age and maturity, the wishes of the child as to legal decision-making and parenting time.
5. The mental and physical health of all individuals involved.
6. Which parent is more likely to allow the child frequent, meaningful and continuing contact with the other parent. This paragraph does not apply if the court determines that a parent is acting in good faith to protect the child from witnessing an act of domestic violence or being a victim of domestic violence or child abuse.
7. Whether one parent intentionally misled the court to cause an unnecessary delay, to increase the cost of litigation or to persuade the court to give a legal decision-making or a parenting time preference to that parent.
8. Whether there has been domestic violence or child abuse pursuant to A.R.S. § 25-403.03.
9. The nature and extent of coercion or duress used by a parent in obtaining an agreement regarding legal decision-making or parenting time.
10. Whether a parent has complied with A.R.S. §§ 25-351 et seq. (addressing domestic relations education on children's issues).
11. Whether either parent was convicted of an act of false reporting of child abuse or neglect under A.R.S. § 13-2907.02 The court may order sole legal decision-making or joint legal decision-making; however, joint legal decision-making generally will not be awarded in cases of domestic violence or other unfavorable circumstances. If the child's parents cannot agree on a plan for legal decision-making or parenting time, each parent must submit a proposed parenting plan, and the court

will determine unagreed issues. In addition, the court will make an order regarding child support, and may specify one parent as the primary caretaker of the child and one home as the primary home of the child for the purposes of defining eligibility for public assistance.

What this means is that the facts that you want to present must be tied to a specific factor. For instance, if you want to present evidence that mom is materialistic and self-centered, you may offer this evidence under factor 5, the mental and physical health of the parties.

Parenting Plans

The Arizona statute on parenting plans continues by saying "if the parents cannot agree on legal decision-making or parenting plans, then each must submit a proposed parenting plan."

At the very least, Arizona requires that you include:

1. Each parent's rights and responsibilities for the personal care, health care, education and religious training.

    Personal care is a new term courtesy of the January 1, 2013 changes. We can surmise that personal care relates to haircuts, clothing style, piercings, and hair dye. Now, with this fourth category of legal decision-making, we can give final authority of certain categories to mom, and other final decision making authority to dads. If religion and education are important to you, why not let the other parent have the "final decision making authority" on health and personal care? It doesn't have to be all or nothing anymore.

2. A schedule of parenting time including a holiday and school break schedule. Many parents do not want a specific schedule. They are afraid if they make changes or do not exercise all parenting time that they may be subject to sanction, and would therefore prefer a plan that called for "reasonable" or "liberal" parenting time. This won't really work under the statute. The Court wants a well though-out, specific plan. With that being said, there is nothing stopping parents from agreeing to modify the plan or from being flexible with the plan.

3. A procedure for exchanges, including who provides transportation, where and when exchanges will take place.

Who, what, where, when and how details are all important when figuring out exchanges. However, understand the spirit of the plan. Just because the plan says mom and dad are to exchange at McDonalds, doesn't mean you can with- hold the children when Aunt Alice comes on behalf of Dad. It's his time, he can generally choose who transports on his behalf as his agent, unless the Court has specified otherwise.

4. A procedure by which proposed changes, disputes and alleged breaches may be mediated or resolved, which may include the use of conciliation services or private counseling.

    This is typically a generic provision requiring mediation prior to bringing an action for modification.

5. A procedure for periodic review of the plan's terms by the parents.

    This is a great idea. It encourages the parents to talk about what is working for their children and them and what isn't. It encourages parents to be cooperative and flexible, which is what the court wants! The Legislature also recognized that one parenting plan or legal order, will rarely satisfy the needs of the children and parents over the long term as children change and relationships develop. Because of that, parents will be required to meet on an annual basis to work out parenting time schedules.

When and if this meeting happens, both parents should bring all documentation to this meeting:

- their work schedules,
- the children's school calendar,
- extracurricular and vacation schedules.

Both parents should be diligent about sending school reports, medical records to the other parent; encourage the children to communicate with the other parent. Each parent should show respect for the other in front of the children—constant sniping or criticism of the absent parent might be construed as alienating behaviors, which sometimes warrants a change in parenting time in favor of the non-alienating parent.

6. A procedure for communicating with each other about the child, including methods and frequency.

More and more, judges are ordering parents to communicate prior to each exchange, either with an email, a notebook that goes back and forth or a worksheet similar to what a day care might provide after a day with a child. The theme here is that courts want parents CO-PARENTING. They want both parents fully engaged in the daily activities of their children's lives and they are moving away from the once typical Disney dads who have every other weekend. Instead of deciding where a kindergartener should attend school, Florence with dad or Gilbert with mom, the Court is telling parents to send the child to school in Queen Creek and meet in the middle. The Court wants each parent to have time with a child during the week and on weekends.

This can be very difficult for some parents. My advice here is that no one is better able make decisions about your children than you are. If you know that equal time isn't good for your child, I urge you to work with the other parent to reach an agreement.

In sum, the court will order a plan that is in the best interest of the child, but they assume that the best interest of the child is equal parenting time. If that isn't the case for you, we need to gather strong evidence to prove that is the case.

Temporary Custody

The court can make an order for temporary custody whenever a Petition for Dissolution or Petition to Establish is pending with the court. Many times, a parent will call and let us know they have been police looking to get assistance with seeing their children. However, until a petition is filed in court, the court has absolutely no jurisdiction to tell you and your spouse how to parent, and they will not enter a temporary order, and the police will not get involved.

After a petition is filed, absent a temporary order, both parents are deemed to be custodial parents, yet neither of them can remove the child from the state, due to the immediate and automatic preliminary injunction that goes into place when the initial petition is filed. This injunction also prevents the parents from interfering with one another, harassing, threatening, or molesting or disturbing the peace of the parent or the child. This won't help a parenting time dispute or help determine where a kiddo should go to school. If there is disagreement to major issues or parenting time, a temporary order may be the only thing that helps.

Are you eligible for ALIMONY?

STEP 1: HAVE ONE OR MORE QUALIFICATIONS

The spouse seeking alimony – called "maintenance" or "spousal support" must first show he or she qualifies by proving any ONE of the following:

- UNABLE TO BE SELF SUFFICIENT
- LACKS PROPERTY TO PROVIDE FOR SELF SUFFICIENCY
- HELPED EX WITH SCHOOL OR CAREER OPPORTUNITIES
- LONG-MARRIED AND PAST THE AGE OF EMPLOYABILITY
- HAS LIMITED EARNING ABILITY

STEP 2: ANALYZE THE FACTORS

If the court agrees one of the qualifiers has been established, ALL of the following factors will be considered when awarding the amount and length of time of spousal maintenance:

- CAREER OR EDUCATION CONTRIBUTIONS OF SPOUSE SEEKING SUPPORT
- STANDARD OF LIVING WHILE MARRIED
- ABILITY OF EACH SPOUSE TO CONTRIBUTE TO EDUCATIONAL COSTS OF THE CHILDREN
- HAS THERE BEEN ANY MISHANDLING OF PROPERTY?
- TIME NEEDED TO BE TRAINED FOR JOB
- AGE, EMPLOYMENT HISTORY, EARNING ABILITY OF SPOUSE SEEKING SUPPORT
- ABILITY OF THE PAYEE TO MEET HIS OR HER OWN NEEDS
- COST OF HEALTH INSURANCE FOR EACH
- YEARS MARRIED
- THE FINANCIAL RESOURCES OF EACH SPOUSE

Years In our hypothetical case, Jim wants to eventually be given equal time with his children. Monica has spent the vast majority of the time with the kids as he spent long hours working to support their lifestyle. He wants a temporary order of equal parenting time so that he doesn't go into a final hearing being deemed an "absent father." He also wants to give Monica plenty of time to go out and look for a job. She will probably claim she can't work if she still has the responsibility for the three kids. Jim will need to make sure that he has adequate housing to have the kids during the pendency of the hearing. He wants to move in with his parents. They have plenty of room and can help him make the transition. His mom would love more time with the kids and both of his parents can offer him support through the transition. We decided to file for a temporary order regarding custody.

When requesting a temporary order, you must file a motion with an accompanying affidavit laying out the facts of why you need a temporary order. If the court is not convinced that a temporary order is necessary, they may deny the motion without a hearing. If the court does believe that the motion warrants a hearing, both parties will be ordered to appear and present their case.

Child Interviews

The court may interview children in chambers of the court. However, most of the time, children are interviewed by a professional, either through conciliation services or by a court appointed professional. When that is the case, the professional must meet requirements of education and training. They may be appointed to interview the children to get their opinion or they may interview the child and use it, among other things, to make recommendations. In Jim's case, the two older girls, Katie and Sarah will likely be interviewed and the youngest, Josh probably will not be interviewed due to his age.

Custody Evaluations

Custody evaluations are now called many different things in Maricopa County. The following is a list of potential experts, who may be involved when there is a custody dispute:

- Parenting conferences
- A psychological evaluation
- A comprehensive family evaluation/assessment
- For a limited family evaluation/Assessment
- Reunification therapy
- Court appointed adviser

The cost of the services can be divided between the parties, born by the party requesting the services, the parent with more resources, or by the court.

Sealing the Record

For confidential or sensitive matters or when parents have a high profile case, they can request that the court seal the record. The court isn't obligated to do so, but the parents may benefit from asking when there are significant issues going on with the kids.

For Jim, his oldest Katie is battling an eating disorder. This will certainly come up in the hearings and in order to protect Katie's privacy, we will ask the court to seal the record.

School Choice/Private School

The court does have the ability to order a child to attend a private religious school and order that both parents pay for it, if it is determined that attending the school is in the child's best interest.

The court MUST make findings under each of the best interest factors in order to make a determination on legal decision making and parenting time.

Model Parenting Plans

You can find model parenting plans developed by various counties all over the Internet. These plans are usually offered as examples and for guidance only. In Arizona, the court must make specific findings and create a parenting plan in the best interest of the children based on those findings. With that being said these model guides pro- vide information as to the developmental needs of children based on their age, the distance between the parties, siblings, and the relationship of the children to each parent. These guidelines can be used as evidence to the court of why your parenting plan might be in the best interest of the children. Alternatively this is an excellent guide for parents who want to develop their own parenting plan for their children. Here is the comprehensive guide offered by the Arizona courts.

http://www.azcourts.gov/portals/31/parentingtime/ppwguidelines.pdf

What is reasonable Parenting Time?

At least one judge has found in a court of appeals case that when a reasonable parenting time is not specified, the model guidelines can provide the parameters for what constitutes reasonable parenting time.

Parenting Time and Child Support

Previously, the court conditioned parenting time on the payment of child support. That is no longer the case. Now, a child is entitled to parenting time with each parent. Parenting time is for the primary benefit of the child and not the parent. It would now be inappropriate to condition parenting time upon the payment of child support.

With that being said, the court has required a parent to bear the cost of transportation in order to exercise out-of-state parenting time, and in another case, has required parent to post a bond prior to the removal of the child from the state for parenting time.

Supervised Parenting Time

Sometimes, the court will order supervised parenting time. In that case, the standard of proof is not whether or not it is in the best interest of the child that the parenting time be supervised. Instead the court must determine that without supervision the children's health or emotional development would be significantly impaired or the child's physical mental moral or emotional health would be seriously in danger, but for supervised parenting time.

Supervised parenting time may take place anywhere. Many times the judge will order that a family member or close friend provide supervision. For instance, it's not unusual for judge to order that a parent have supervised parenting time where their parents (the grandparents) act as the supervisor, when a child has an established relationship with the grandparents and the court has no reason to doubt that the child will be safe and healthy the supervision of grandparents. Alternatively, if the parties cannot agree on an appropriate supervisor or there is no friend or family supervisor willing to supervise parenting time, the court will order that an agency provide supervised parenting time. The court will determine who will bear the cost of the supervision. It may be split between the parties, paid by one party, or paid by the court.

Video or Skype parenting time

In this day and age, it is not unusual for a court to order Skype or other video parenting time especially for young children or when the parents live in different states from one another. This can prove very difficult for the party who is expected to facilitate the Skype parenting time. It is not unusual for young children to be resistant or rambunctious or rowdy during scheduled Skype parenting time. It can also be difficult to coordinate a time when a parent always must be home and available to coordinate the video parenting time.

Custody to Non-parents

The court may order visitation or custody to nonparents, like grandparents or other third parties, in unusual and appropriate circumstances. Third-party visitation is not considered parenting time. Third party visitation cannot be granted during a divorce or paternity proceeding. In order to be eligible for third-party custody or visitation, the grandparents or other third party must file a petition to establish third-party rights (either custody or visitation).

The petitioner requesting custody must prove that they have stood "in loco parentis" or "in the shoes of the parent" and that they have acted as the child's parent. This relationship does not have to be to the detriment of the actual parents relationship, but the petitioner must prove that their relationship with the child was a meaningful parental relationship for substantial period of time.

In addition to proving that the person filing stood in loco parentis they must also plead facts that indicate it would be significantly detrimental to the child to remain, or to be placed in the care of either legal parent, that a court has not entered or approved a conflicting order of legal custody within one year and that one of the following conditions has been met:

1. One of the legal parents is deceased;
2. The child's legal parents are not married to each other when petition filed, or;
3. A proceeding for divorce or legal separation is pending and petition for third party rights is filed.

There is a presumption that legal parents are fit to have custody and to make decisions about who their child see and when. Grandparent or third-party visitation is not granted immediately or as a matter of right. In fact, the third party must show by clear and convincing evidence that granting custody to The parents is not in the children's best interest.

Third Party Visitation

In order to get third-party visitation the standard is a bit lower. A third party may petition the court for visitation if any of the following conditions have been met:

1. One of the legal parents is deceased or has been missing for three months or more,
2. The child was born out of wedlock and the child's legal parents are not married to each other at the time the petition for visitation is filed,
3. For grandparent for great grandparent visitation, the marriage of the parents of the child needed to have been dissolved for at least three months

When filing a petition for third-party custody, official notice needs to be provided to the children's legal parents, a person or agency that has physical custody of the child or claims any sort of custodial rights, or any other person or agency that has previously appeared in a court case.

Parents are granted special weight in their opinions when the court decides cases involving third parties. The court is also instructed to consider the historical relation- ship between the child and the third party seeking visitation, the motivation of the person who is seeking and requesting visitation, and the motivation of the person who is objecting to the visitation. Additionally, the court is instructed to look at the child's customary activities and weigh the potential benefits and risks of harm to the child customary activities like sports, or other extra-curricular activities.

When one parent dies, the court is particularly concerned with protecting the child's relationship to his or her deceased parent's parents, or the grandparents of the child. The court wants to preserve that extended family relationship. When these facts are present, it seems easier to get the court to grant third-party visitation.

Once visitation has been established it is not terminated if a parent chooses to relocate out of the state. That parent is still responsible to ensure that the child gets visitation with his or her grandparents or other third party. If the order for visitation is ignored the parent may be subject to contempt proceedings. With that being said, a parent does not need the permission of the court or the third party/grandparents in order to relocate with the child.

Relocation

The Relocation cases can be very tricky. Let's go back to our example with Jim and Monica. If Monica wants to move to Oregon then she must follow the procedures set out in ARS 25 – 408. If Jim and Monica have agreed to joint legal decision-making, and Monica wants to move out of the state, she must provide Jim with at least 60 days advance written notice that she wants to relocate either outside the state or within the state more than 100 miles away. If she fails to provide this written notice, certified mail return receipt requested, she may be subject to sanctions by the court, and may lose joint legal decision-making.

Once Jim has received notice that Monica wants to move to Oregon, he has 30 days to file a petition with the court to prevent the relocation of the child. If he fails to file this petition then Monica may file a petition to relocate. She will have to prove to the court that the relocation benefits outweigh the adverse impact upon the relationship of her children and Jim.

Assuming that the relocation is permitted by the court, all of the other orders remain in effect. If there's a parenting time provision that Jim gets the children for the third week of every month, Monica must deliver to Jim the children for the third week of every month, regardless of whether or not she is currently in Oregon.

Where do we count the miles?

If we are trying to determine whether we have breached the 100 mile radius required under the relocation statute, a necessary question is from where do we count the miles. A recent court of appeals decision states that we count the 100 miles starting from where the relocating parent was at that time the court order was initially entered.

Emergency Relocation

Now let's say something has happened to Monica. She's got a new boyfriend, Bob, who is supporting her and the kids. Let's say Bob becomes violent and he kicks her and the children out of the home. If Monica has either sole legal decision-making or joint legal decision-making but has the children most of the time and is deemed the "primary residential parent", she may be able to relocate on a temporary basis. The statute allows that apparently sole legal decision-making or joint legal decision-making and primary residence as required by circumstances of health, safety, employment or eviction of that parent or that parents spouse to relocate in less than 60 days after the written notice has been given.

Even under the emergency relocation provision, if Jim and Monica have joint legal decision-making and substantially equal parenting time, Monica may only leave before her 45-day time frame if Jim agrees.

The Relocation Hearing

If the parents are unable to agree to the relocation, and the court must make a decision of whether or not to allow a parent to relocate more than 100 miles away from the parent or out-of-state, the parent who is proposing the relocation has the burden of proving that the relocation is in the best interest of the child. The court is specifically instructed to make appropriate arrangements to ensure a continuing meaningful relationship between the child and both parents.

In addition to the best interest factors above, the court also looks at whether the relocation proposal is being made in good faith or whether it is intended to interfere with or frustrate the relationship between the child and the other parent. The court will also examine whether or not the proposed move may affect the amount of child support the moving party stands to gain in diminishing the other parents parenting time. The court also looks that the prospective advantage of the move to improve the general quality-of-life for the custodial parent or child. Interestingly, the statute also instructs the court to look at the likelihood that the parent moving the child out of state will comply with future parenting time orders, and whether the relocation will allow a realistic opportunity quality time with each parent.

Fundamentally, the court will assess the potential effect of the relocation on the child's stability and extent to which moving or not moving will affect the emotional, physical, or developmental needs of the child.

The relocation statute also includes an interesting provision, that has more to do with contempt then it does relocation.

Contempt of Court

ARS section 25-408J States that the court **shall** assess attorney fees and court costs against either parent if the court finds that the parent has unreasonably denied, restricted, or interfered with court-ordered parenting time.

That means it is not optional for the court to award fees. If we are able to prove in a content proceeding that a parent has recently denied, restricted, or interfered you're your parenting time, you will be reimbursed for your attorney fees and court costs associated with securing the contact.

Notes

Chapter 10
Child Support

How Does It Work? How Much Will It Cost?

Child support affects all divorced or unmarried parents of minor children, including adopted children. Many people have questions about how the child support obligation is determined and what to do when child support isn't appropriate in their case.

Parents' obligation to pay child support takes priority over all other financial obligations, which is why parents may be thrown in jail for failing to pay child support. No other failure to pay a financial obligation carries such a steep penalty. A parent may not claim the protection of bankruptcy or seek forgiveness of unpaid child support. As a matter of principle, many parents would prefer to pay directly for things their children need instead of giving money to the other parent. However, child support must be paid in cash, not gifts or payment of direct expenses.

The basic premise for determining a child support obligation is to determine what portion of each parent's income would have been spent for the benefit of the child if the parents were living together. Obviously, there is a huge variation in how much parents spend on their children, so it is understandable that the guidelines would sometimes come up with numbers far different than what you would spend in your household.

As a starting point, the federal guidelines are based on a 2009 report from the Center for Policy Research, http://www.centerforpolicyresearch.org/ a private nonprofit research agency based in Denver. Every four years each state is required to review and update the guidelines based on changes in the cost-of-living. In Arizona, the child support guidelines changed on July 1, 2015 to provide a higher self-support reserve for the paying parent.

Why even have child support guidelines given that families are so different?

- To establish a standard of support for the children of parents who are not together.
- To make support orders consistent.
- To give parents' and courts' guidance in establishing the child support (promote settlement).

With all that being said, the child support guidelines create only a presumption. If a judge decides the child support amount is unjust or unreasonable in a certain case, or the parents decide the child support guidelines should not be applied to them, the judge can order a different amount. In fact, the guidelines state "if application of the guidelines would be inappropriate or unjust in a given case, the court SHALL deviate from the guidelines."

When does child support end?

In Arizona, child support ends when the youngest child turns 18 and graduates from high school. If the child has not graduated from high school at 18, child support will last until the child turns 19 (rounded up to the end of the month).

This is not the case in many other states. Some states require a parent to pay child support while they are in college. If your child support order began in another state, it may continue through college. This is certainly something to check with an attorney about.

It is also possible to receive child support for a disabled child beyond the age of 18. For this issue you will definitely want to consult with an attorney.

What counts as income for child support purposes?

To determine your income and the opposing party's income for the child support calculator, you should include income from all sources, including:

- Income from salaries

- Wages
- Commissions
- Bonuses
- Dividends
- Severance pay
- Trust income
- Workers' Compensation benefits
- Annuities
- Capital gains
- Spousal maintenance
- Unemployment insurance benefits
- Disability insurance benefits, including social security disability benefits.

This is not an exhaustive list, meaning that just because a particular income source isn't listed here doesn't mean it won't be included as income for child support purposes.

What is excluded as income?

- Child support
- Food stamps (the SNAP program)
- Temporary Assistance for Needy Families (TANF)
- Supplemental Security Income (SSI) (money given to low income individuals who have never worked or who haven't worked enough to accumulate benefits.)

What about overtime, seasonal work or other income that is uncertain for the future?

Sometimes people work a lot of overtime in a certain season. Accountants work more hours during tax season than the rest of the year; certainly they should not be made to work 80 hours a week all year only to pay for child support. Or, consider a person who works many overtime hours during the Christmas season at UPS. They cannot be expected to continue to earn income at that rate throughout the year.

The guidelines state the court should not consider overtime. Each parent should have the choice of working additional hours through overtime or a second job with- out increasing child support, except if that overtime was historically earned and is anticipated to continue in future. Seems a bit contradictory, doesn't it?

This means usual or expected overtime can be considered when determining child support, but not when overtime would require an extraordinary work regimen. This must be determined given the actual facts of the case, the occupation, and the working hours and conditions involved.

For instance, firefighters might work four twenty-four hour shifts and then have four days off. This is the schedule for all firefighters in that division and is expected to continue. The firefighter always received overtime and is always expected to work overtime. Their income, including any overtime pay, should be included in the child support calculation.

On the other hand, consider a restaurant server. A server may be working an average of five shifts per week. During spring training, they may end up working eight to ten shifts per week. The courts should not assume the server will continue to work eight to ten shifts per week and should instead attribute a reasonable average when determining the income of that parent.

How do I find out how much my ex makes?

In any case, each party must provide an Affidavit of Financial Information. Typically, this provides all the information you need. In some cases, it is not enough and you need to use additional discovery tools to find the information you need.

Once a child support order is entered, the court is required to order that the parties exchange financial information like tax returns and earning statements. You are also required to exchange residential addresses and the names and addresses of employers. If there have been significant changes in income or other factors, you may want to seek a modification.

What if the parent is self-employed or owns a business?

Business owners have a great deal of control over what they pay themselves as income. It can be very difficult to determine the correct amount to use for child support purposes. It wouldn't be fair to consider all of the income earned by a business as income to a parent, just as it wouldn't be fair to consider only the net number after all expenses have been paid.

For income from self-employment, rent on a rental property, or joint ownership in a business, income is considered to be gross revenue (all money brought in the door) minus ordinary and necessary business expenses. Often, the best starting place is income on tax returns. However, this is only a starting place. A parent may be able to deduct expenses for tax purposes that should not be deducted for child support purposes. For instance, payment for a car or phone or internet at your house may be deductible for IRS purposes, but should not be deducted for child support purposes because all parents typically have the cost of cars, phones and internet.

What if a parent is voluntarily unemployed or underemployed?

If a parent is unemployed or underemployed, the court has the discretion to consider the reasons. The court should look to whether the underemployment is reasonable. A mom with a newborn could reasonably take time off or reduce her workload. A father who moves to be closer to his children may voluntarily reduce income while seeking new state licensure. This could be reasonable under the circumstances. The court should weigh the costs and benefits of the parent's choice and the reduction of child support in light of what is in the best interest of the children.

Income of at least minimum wage for full-time employment should be attributed to both parents. With that being said, if a parent is home taking care of small children and the court attributes wages to that parent, make sure and ask the court to also at- tribute the child care costs associated with full-time work. There are circumstances when a court need not attribute income to a parent. Examples might include:

- A mentally or physically disabled parent
- A full-time student (if the court determines the schooling is reasonably calcu-lated to enhance earning capacity)
- Extraordinary emotional or physical needs of a child that require a parent to stay home to care for the child

If the court attributes or imputes income higher than minimum wage, the court must make findings on the record and explain the reasons for the decision to at- tribute the income.

What about the income of roommates or new spouses?

Only the income of both parents will be considered when calculating child support. Since only legal parents have the legal responsibility to support the child, other sources of support like grandparents, new spouses, or roommate contributions will not be considered. The amount of property a parent owns will not be considered unless the property produces income.

What about income taxes and other non-voluntary reductions in pay?

Child support obligations are based on net income. The impact of taxes has been considered. If you are in a position where non-voluntary reductions of pay extend beyond typical taxes, you will want to make sure to bring this to the attention of the court.

People who work for the state of Arizona are required to contribute 11.5% of their income into a non-voluntary retirement system. People employed by the state should consider asking the court to factor in this non-voluntary contribution when deter- mining child support.

Other than income, what else is considered when determining child support?

1. **Other Children**

   Non-joint children or "children of other relationships" refers to your legal children who are not subject to this child support order. Your obligation to support your other children is factored into your overall child support obligation to each child. To determine the amount of the deduction, you can look to the tables and find your income and the corresponding cost for the number of children you have.

2. **Court-ordered child support**

Additionally, if you are paying child support to other children, that court-ordered support is deducted from your income as non-available to pay to the cur- rent child.

3. **Court-ordered spousal maintenance**

Spousal maintenance paid is deducted from income by the paying parent and attributed to the income of anyone receiving spousal maintenance. Arrearages (unpaid amounts owed) are not deducted or included. That means if you are re-ceiving $500 per month spousal maintenance and an additional $200 in arrears owed to you, your income (in the child support calculator) will only increase by the $500 court-ordered maintenance amount.

After the incomes of both parents are established, the court determines the overall child support obligation based on the combined income. The maximum combined income that is considered is $20,000. Then the court determines the proportion that each parent should contribute.

Note: If you would like the court to consider income above $20,000, you will have the burden of proving the standard of living the children would have enjoyed if the family lived together, and any additional expenses of the children, that would create a need for increased child support. Essentially, the court has the ability to order an upward deviation based on income over $20,000. But if you are seeking this deviation, you must prove that it is appropriate in your case. This is to avoid a child support obligation of $10,000 a month from an NBA superstar to his mistress, for example.

After the basic obligation is determined, other factors will modify the total child support amount.

The cost of medical insurance

The cost to insure the child for medical, dental and vision insurance is added to the initial obligation. <u>This is not discretionary</u>. Notice this is only the cost to insure the child. As an example, if it costs $100 for the mother to insure herself, and an additional $100 to insure all dependents, the cost of medical insurance for one child would be one hundred dollars divided by the number of dependents.

Who pays for health insurance?

The order for child support should include an order of who must provide health insurance for the children. To determine who must provide insurance, the court will look at who has the ability to provide insurance either through their employer or another source. If both parents can and want to provide insurance, the court will usually order the custodial parent or the parent who has more time with the children to provide insurance.

Who pays for uncovered medical expenses?

The court will also specify what portion of uncovered medical expenses each party must pay. Only medically necessary medical expenses are subject to reimbursement from the parent who got the services. What is medically necessary is subject to much debate and is decided on a case-by-case basis.

How do I seek reimbursement?

Generally speaking, a parent must provide the request for reimbursement of the uninsured costs within six months or 180 days of the date of services. The other parent should then pay his or her share within 45 days of the receipt of the request. The guidelines do not state that the parent who provided the medical coverage must provide receipts, only that they must request payment. However, the parent should be prepared to provide receipts of the actual services rendered.

What if one parent does not use services covered by insurance?

Each parent is required to use their best efforts to obtain services covered by insurance. If a parent has used non-covered medical services, then actual receipts of services are required to be provided to the other parent.

Discretionary adjustments to the child support obligation

1. Childcare costs

In practice, courts almost always consider childcare costs when determining the child support obligation. Based on the rules, this is discretionary, meaning the judge does not have to adjust child support based on the cost of childcare. When determining whether the childcare costs are appropriate, the judge will look at the parents' financial abilities. For instance, it would not be appropriate for a parent who is earning $10 an hour to hire a nanny at $10 an hour.

The court also considers that a parent paying for childcare will be entitled to a federal tax credit. The court is specifically authorized to adjust the childcare costs based on who will be receiving the tax credit.

Additionally, the court should take the childcare costs and average them throughout the year. Many people have increased childcare costs during the summer when the children are not in school. Consider adding up what you spend on childcare during the entire year and dividing it by 12 when using the child support calculator.

Educational Expenses

Educational expenses, like the cost of private school, tutoring, or special educational classes outside of the regular school day, can be considered when determining child support. However, one parent may not unilaterally decide to sign up a child for Japanese lessons and seek reimbursement. These activities need to be agreed upon by both parents or ordered by the court.

Extraordinary Child Expenses

Remember, the guidelines were designed with the average child in mind and the expenses associated with that child. If your child has extraordinary needs and there- fore extraordinary expenses, you can ask that the court adjust the child support obligation in accordance with these special needs.

Older Child Adjustment

Children over the age of 12 cost more than children under 12 by about 10%. The court can adjust the basic obligation by 10% for all children over the age of 12. For instance, if the child support obligation for a 14-year-old is $400, the court can increase the obligation to $440 due to the child's age. If the total obligation for three children is $1200 and one is over the age of 12, the court would add 10% only for the older child (1200/3 = 400)(400 + 10% = $440). The total obligation would be $1240.

What is each parent's responsibility?

At this point, we have determined the overall obligation to support the child. Both parents share the responsibility of support, so the overall number will be allocated between the parents in proportion to their income. For example, if Mother earns 60% of the combined income, she will be responsible for 60% of the $1240 obligation described above.

Parenting Time Adjustments

Up until this point, we have only determined what percentage of each parent's income should be spent to support their joint children, with no adjustment for who actually pays the expenses. The parenting time credit seeks to ensure that the custodial parent is reimbursed for the day-to-day expenses incurred.

In order to calculate the number of days that a non-custodial parent has the child, the court adds together the various blocks of time the parent spends with the child. A block of time starts when the parent receives or returns the child from school, childcare, or the custodial parent. As a general rule, a non-custodial parent is not credited for time the child is in childcare or school. A period of 12 or more hours with the non-custodial parent is one day, 6 to 11 hours is a half-day, 3 to 5 hours is a quarter-day, and 3 hours or less could be a quarter-day if the parent is providing for routine expenses like meals. This is an attempt to be fair if you have a non-custodial parent who is providing afterschool care for the child up until bedtime every day.

For example, if the parent picks up a child at school at 3 o'clock Friday and then drops her child off at school on Monday morning, the parenting time credit would be 2.5 days.

Once the total number of days is determined, the support obligation is adjusted according to parenting timetables A and B, which can be found in the child support guidelines.

If parenting time is equal, no adjustments are made and the child-support obligation is shared in proportion to the parents' income.

Self-support Reserve

As we mentioned, the self-support reserve was increased when the 2015 child sup- port guidelines were modified. Even though child support is considered a parent's primary financial obligation, the self-support reserve test is to make sure that the non-custodial parent can take care of himself or herself at a minimum standard of living. For parents with very minimal income, the child support obligation will be adjusted down to account for their self-support reserve.

Divided Custody

Sometimes parents with multiple children will have divided custody, meaning each parent may be the primary custodial parent to one or more of the children. When that is the case, create two child support calculations and determine the difference. For instance, if the mother has primary custody of one child and the father has primary custody of one child, you can prepare two child support worksheets (one for each parent) that each assume one joint child. The difference between the amounts owed will be the child support ordered.

Travel Expenses

Travel expenses are not factored into the child support calculator or obligation. They must be assigned to the parents separately, either in a divorce decree or a parenting plan/custody decree.

Child Support Deviations

A deviation from the child support guidelines occurs when either the judge orders, or the parties agree to, an amount that is different from the guidelines explained here.

The judge can accept a deviation that has been agreed to by the parties only if the parties have entered into a binding Rule 69 agreement, with the knowledge of what the child support would have been under the guidelines.

The court can deviate from the guidelines after they have considered all factors and they meet the statutory requirements. A judge must make findings on the record as follows:

1. That the guidelines are inappropriate or unjust in a particular case.
2. That the court has considered the best interest of the child or children in determining the amount of the deviation.
3. That the court has completed the child support worksheet and has considered the presumptive amount under the worksheet and after the deviation.

In fact, the court must make findings in all child support orders regarding the gross income of both parties, the adjusted gross incomes, the basic child support obligation, the total child support obligation, and each parent's proportionate share of the child support obligation. If the judge includes a child support worksheet, it is assumed that the numbers used in the worksheet(s) constitute the judge's findings.

What if the child doesn't live with either parent?

Sometimes a child may live with grandparents or other third-party caregivers. In that event, those third-party caregivers are entitled to receive child support from the legal parents according to the guidelines explained here. In order to receive the support, the third party must seek a child support order from the court by filing a petition for child support and naming both the legal mother and father in court action. The third party would then be required to appear in court or get a stipulated judgment for child support.

IV-D cases

If the office of child support enforcement (DCS or Division of Child Support) is involved in your case, you have a IV-D case. That means the state is a party to the action and must be served on all court paperwork, including modifications of child support.

Modifications of Child Support

There are two ways to seek a modification of child support, the standard and simplified procedures.

Standard Procedure:

Through the standard procedure, either parent or the state may request a modification by alleging and proving a substantial and continuing change of circumstances. A change in circumstances could be due to a parenting time change, a relocation, change in incomes of the parties, birth or adoption of additional children, or any combination of the factors outlined here.

Simplified Procedure:

The simplified procedure allows a party to request a modification of an order based on a change that would cause child support to change by 15% or more. This is evidence in and of itself of a substantial and continuing change in circumstances. Your petition to modify must be accompanied by a completed child support worksheet and supporting documentation of the figures used in the worksheet titled

"Parent's Worksheet for Child Support Amount." If you don't have documentation, don't worry; you may still request the modification and simply indicate to the court your estimate and the basis for the estimate.

After you file documents and serve the other party, you don't have to do anything. The other parent is required to request a hearing within 20 days if within the state of Arizona, or 30 days if the parent lives out of state. If no hearing is requested, the court will either modify the child support with the information provided within the petition, or will set a hearing. If either party requests a hearing, one will be set before child support is modified.

If you have multiple children, you must seek a modification of child support when one of your children turns 18 and graduates from high school. The child support obligation is not automatically reduced by that child's proportion of the amount.

Federal Tax Exemption

Parents can claim the federal and state tax exemptions for their minor children according to their agreement. If the parents do not agree, then the court will deter- mine who may claim the federal exemption based on each parent's adjusted gross income. If both parties have substantially similar gross incomes, they may alternate every other year on who claims the tax exemption. If Father earns twice as much as Mother, he may claim the child two out of every three years. This is very frustrating for many parents, especially the custodial parent who may earn less. However, it is designed to maximize the communal benefit to all parties. If a parent is behind in paying child support, they are typically prohibited from claiming any tax exemption.

Child Support Arrears

Child support arrears occur when a parent has not paid all of the court-ordered child support. The amount owed is called the arrears. The court will set not only your child support obligation, but also a payment on the arrears balance, which accrues monthly interest. If a child turns 18, which is when the child support obligation would typically end, but a parent owes arrears, that parent's child support obligations will continue until the total amount owed (arrearage) is paid.

Notes

Chapter 11
Spousal Maintenance

Spousal maintenance, formerly known as alimony, refers to cash support paid by one spouse to the other. For a spouse that needs alimony to survive on a monthly basis, this could be the most important issue faced during the divorce. In the past, alimony could only be requested by a wife, to be paid by her husband. This is no longer the case. Now, either spouse may request spousal maintenance if they qualify under the statute.

For an order to constitute an award of maintenance, specific language need not be included. Any monthly support payments that are not for the purpose of dividing property can be spousal maintenance. This is important because of the tax consequences associated with maintenance; these will be discussed below.

Spousal maintenance cases can be some of the most difficult to navigate. At Modern Law, we have secured indefinite spousal maintenance awards, interim or temporary spousal maintenance awards, and have successfully defended against and defeated unjust spousal maintenance claims. While the law offers parameters, a skilled lawyer is essential is often needed when navigating the treacherous waters of spousal maintenance.

Many people call it "alimony" or "spousal support," but A.R.S. § 25-319 refers to sup- port of a spouse as "maintenance." There are probably more misconceptions sur- rounding spousal maintenance than any other area of law. Here, it pays to know the law and to plead correctly in your initial documents.

If you are entitled to spousal maintenance and fail to request it in your petition, you may need go back and amend your petition in order to seek maintenance.

Similarly, if you waive spousal maintenance in a divorce proceeding, you cannot go back and modify your divorce decree to seek spousal maintenance. You will definitely want to seek advice and counsel on these issues before proceeding.

You have only one opportunity to get this issue correct. While you can always change a custody/parenting time decree to fit with the best interests of the child, you cannot go back and get spousal maintenance if it is not awarded in the divorce decree.

The Affidavit of Financial Information

In a spousal maintenance case, you should take your Affidavit of Financial Information VERY seriously and walk through each item carefully and strategically. The ramifications of this document can be crucial in a spousal maintenance case. Also, it is important to be accurate. You and your spouse will turn over bank statements, credit card statements and other financial documents to each other. If your documents do not match your Affidavit of Financial Information, it could have serious consequences.

The AFI is required in EVERY case that involves any type of financial issue like child support and spousal maintenance. In this document, you are providing your gross monthly income from all sources, monthly expenses, information regarding the children you support, and any other person or persons who reside in your house- hold and are employed.

You will need documentation of your monthly finances such as:

- Recent pay stubs and any other documentation showing other sources of income
- Information regarding your children
- Information regarding other people residing in your household
- Information regarding your current and past employers
- Your last 3 years' income tax returns
- Information regarding self-employment if applicable
- A list of all of your monthly expenses
- Information regarding costs of medical/dental/vision insurance
- Information regarding costs of childcare if applicable
- List of debts with amounts owed and minimum payments required

You must do the best you can to provide accurate information for this document. Please be aware that you MUST provide this document to the opposing party in your case. It MUST have attached your last 2 pay stubs and the last 3 years' income tax returns for all jobs you had during those tax years with W-2 and 1099 forms included. The first page of the document must be signed. This document must be filed with the court and a complete copy given to the judge assigned to your case.

Temporary Spousal Maintenance

A spouse can seek temporary spousal maintenance by filing a motion for temporary orders requesting maintenance. This motion is accompanied by an affidavit laying out all the facts for why the maintenance is needed. The motion should address cur- rent living expenses, the lack of funds to pay the expenses through employment or savings, or the lack of access to community funds, and it should address the other spouse's ability to pay temporary maintenance.

The motion should also include expenses associated with the divorce, like attorney's fees or moving expenses.

The responding spouse will be served an order to appear for a temporary orders hearing. For more information on a temporary orders hearing, click here.

For both temporary orders and a permanent award of spousal maintenance, the analysis is the same. (With that being said, different judges treat this differently. At least one Maricopa County judge splits the income in half on a temporary basis, pending the divorce trial.)

The statutory analysis is as follows:

First Step: Qualification

The spouse seeking maintenance must show he or she qualifies by documenting any one of the following:

- Property, including property received in the divorce, is insufficient to provide for his or her reasonable needs;

- The spouse is unable to be self-sufficient through appropriate work, or lacks enough earning ability in the labor market to be self-sufficient, or takes care of a child whose age or condition requires the spouse to not work outside the home;
- The spouse contributed to the educational or career opportunities of the other spouse; or
- The marriage was for long duration and the spouse is of an age that prevents them from employment adequate to be self-sufficient.

If you do not pass this step, or your spouse cannot qualify under one of these factors, the court does not get to step two. This initial analysis is arguably the most important analysis to your case.

A few things should be noted here regarding the first factor above: When consider- ing the amount of property that one spouse will receive, we are not stating that that spouse must use up all of the property in order to meet his or her reasonable needs. Instead, the court is looking at the income that the property is able to produce as a consideration for whether the spouse can provide for his or her reasonable needs. The court is actually required to consider the "income-earning potential" of the property awarded to the spouse.

When looking at the second factor (self-sufficiency through work), the court is not looking at speculative expectations of employment, but rather actual employment or the ability to become employed. For instance, if a person must seek licensure before they can begin working, then they are not currently able to be self-sufficient through appropriate employment. We would also look at the health of the spouse when considering whether or not he or she is able to be self-sufficient through employment. The court will also look at the efforts (or lack of efforts) the spouse has made to become employed during the pendency of the divorce. This can be particularly challenging, because the spouse is often going through a great deal of stress and transition during this time. This can make trying to find a new job or entering the workforce even harder than it would be otherwise. However, the judge will want to know what efforts you have made to become employed when considering whether or not you qualify for maintenance under this factor.

The third factor exists so that a spouse who has supported and contributed to the other spouse's professional degree gets fairly compensated. This is because after the divorce, a degree in law, medicine, pharmacy, or other profession will be the separate property of the spouse who earned the degree.

The fourth factor is usually applied for marriage of a very long duration when spouses are around 50 years old or older. This is typically the scenario for any indefinite awards of maintenance.

Second Step: Analyzing the Factors

Once the court finds the spouse seeking maintenance has established one or more of the above qualifiers, the court must consider the following factors in order to decide how much spousal maintenance to award, and how long it should last. The underlying purpose of spousal maintenance is for both parties to achieve independence and to require an effort toward independence for the spouse who is seeking maintenance. The court will look at whether or not a good faith effort is being made toward achieving independence. The court generally prefers a fixed term of maintenance rather than a lifetime award of maintenance.

In its analysis the court will consider the following:

1. *Standard of living established during the marriage.* Here, the court will also look at whether the standard of living was consistent during the marriage and whether the standard of living was accumulated by acquiring debt. The court recognizes that each spouse cannot necessarily maintain the exact standard of living enjoyed during the marriage, but one spouse shouldn't be required to consume property while the other maintains the former lifestyle through income.

2. *Duration of the marriage.* In general, under 10 years is a short marriage, 10-20 years is a medium length marriage and over 20 years is a marriage of long duration.

3. *Age, employment history, earning ability, and physical and emotional condition of the spouse seeking maintenance.* For this factor, it is the ability to earn and not actual earnings that matter. The facts of the case, including young children, may affect the earning ability of the spouse. Employment history is a factor used to

determine earning ability. The court balances the effort and actual ability for the spouse seeking maintenance to become self-sufficient.

4. *Ability of the spouse requested to pay, to meet his or her own needs while paying maintenance.* This factor considers the separate assets and all available income of the paying spouse, balanced with that spouse's actual expenses, including debt. One case held that an award of less than 25% was certainly within the payor spouse's ability. Future earnings and earning capacity can also be considered, not just what a spouse is actually earning.

5. *Comparative financial resources of the spouses, including their comparative earn- ing abilities in the labor market.* Awards anywhere between 16.5% of the disparity in income all the way up to 47% of the disparity of income have been upheld by the court of appeals.

6. *Contribution of the spouse seeking maintenance to the earning ability of the other spouse.*

7. *Extent to which the maintenance-seeking spouse reduced his or her income or career opportunities for the benefit of the other spouse.* When the issue of maintenance goes before the court, the court looks at the financial status of both spouses. What did one spouse give up while helping the other spouse develop a better career? How much did the working spouse gain because the other spouse did not work to his or her full ability but assisted and supported the working spouse in career advancement?

8. *Ability of both parties after the dissolution to contribute to the future educational costs of their mutual children.* For this factor, it is reasonable to consider the costs both parties have assumed for paying a child's college tuition, books or living expenses. The case on point stated that the husband could be required to pay maintenance to the wife so that that she could also contribute to the childrens' college costs. His reduction in income due to spousal maintenance should be offset by a reduction in his expenses associated with college.

9. *Financial resources of the party seeking maintenance, including marital property awarded in the divorce, and that spouse's ability to meet his or her own needs inde- pendently.* Here, considerations include whether or not liquid assets or income-producing assets would be awarded in the divorce. Also, if a spouse received a home or car, did it come with corresponding debt or are the assets paid off, there- by reducing the need for monthly income? The court should also look at the income that will be received from retirement assets, like IRA or pension income.

10. *Time necessary to acquire sufficient education or training so that the maintenance-seeking spouse may find appropriate employment, and whether such education or training is readily available.* The court will look at whether or not employment should be suggested for the spouse. If a spouse is 65 years old and has not worked during the marriage, then training or employment is probably unlikely. On the other hand, if the spouse seeking maintenance is looking to become a licensed nurse, the court will look at whether the training is available and the time it might take to get the education, license and employment. The court might also look at a person's history in school. Have they historically done well in school or not?

11. *Excessive or abnormal expenditures, destruction, concealment or fraudulent disposition of community, joint tenancy and other property held in common.* Misrepresentation of income and/or hiding assets could result in a spouse paying more spousal maintenance than they otherwise would have.

    As an example, we recently represented a party in a case involving a long-term marriage where one party owned a medical practice. The wife worked in the business and raised the parties' four children. Upon filing for divorce, the doctor stopped working and went to Hawaii with a mistress for three months. The court found that he specifically underperformed in his duties to the medical practice, undervaluing the asset of the practice. The wife was awarded $3,000 per month spousal maintenance forever.

    Spousal maintenance cannot be awarded simply due to waste/concealment if the spouse doesn't qualify for maintenance under one of the first four factors.

12. *Cost for the maintenance-seeking spouse to obtain health insurance and the reduction in the cost of health insurance for the spouse from whom maintenance is sought if the latter is able to convert family health insurance to employee health insurance after the marriage is dissolved.* We all know that the cost of health coverage has skyrocketed in recent years. This factor specifically allows the court to consider the future expense associated with health coverage for a spouse who will be losing their coverage from their spouse. The spouse seeking maintenance should research this and present the evidence to the court?

13. *All actual damages and judgments from conduct that results in criminal conviction of either spouse in which the other spouse or child was the victim.* If your spouse was abusive, this is the only place in family court where civil-type damages may be

awarded. You may have an additional claim for civil damages. Click here to learn more.

You have the right to request "findings of fact." If you make such a request, the court will be required to apply your facts to each and every factor laid out above. If findings of fact are not requested, a judge need not discuss every factor in the ruling and can simply discuss the factors they find applicable.

What Constitutes Income

To determine your income and the opposing party's income for the spousal maintenance analysis, you should include income from all sources, including:

- Income from salaries
- Wages
- Commissions
- Bonuses
- Dividends
- Severance pay
- Trust income
- Workers' Compensation benefits
- Annuities
- Capital gains
- Spousal maintenance
- Unemployment insurance benefits
- Disability insurance benefits, including Social Security Disability benefits.

What isn't Income

Veterans Disability benefits CANNOT be considered income for the purposes of paying spousal maintenance.

Excessive Spending and Marital Misconduct

Factor 11, listed above, requires the court to determine excessive spending, concealing property, or fraud. However, the court will **NOT** consider "marital misconduct," such as extramarital affairs. Any marital misconduct to be considered by the court in a spousal maintenance award must be financially based.

Community waste is a claim during divorce that your spouse wasted community funds and needs to pay you back for spending money on items, people, or services that did not benefit you or your marriage.

For instance, if your husband regularly used a prostitute and paid for these "services" with community funds, you may have a claim for **community waste**. If you prove your husband "wasted" community funds, you are entitled to be reimbursed for half of the expenditures.

If your wife had a gambling problem that you were unaware of, or you did not know the extent of the gambling problem, you may have a claim for community waste. The issue is concealment. If you knew about the gambling, or participated with her, then it will be considered a "recreational cost" and not community waste.

If your spouse had an affair, and purchased gifts or spent money traveling with his or her lover, you may have a claim for waste. You will need to show exactly how much was spent on the affair to establish your claim.

Waste may have an impact on your spousal maintenance claim or defense.

Maricopa County Guidelines

Unlike with the issue of child support, there is no financial calculator used to determine spousal maintenance or even a range of what spousal maintenance might be. Additionally, even when facing the exact same facts, six different judges could end up awarding six different rulings on spousal maintenance. Some may not even agree on whether it should be awarded at all. Here, it pays to have an experienced attorney who knows the judges. More than with any other issue, it may be a good idea to <u>change judges</u> depending on the trends of the judge and your particular position on the issue.

With that being said, the Maricopa County judges came up with a mathematical formula as guidelines to be used AFTER the threshold determination of eligibility has been made. The guidelines are designed to be a point of discussion and not a presumption.

The guidelines are based in part on the following assumed facts:

- That each party's expenses exceed their income;
- The spouse seeking maintenance is not working or works at a wage level which makes it impossible to make a substantial contribution toward the support of the child or children; and
- The payment of support and maintenance comes before all other obligations.

The guidelines are for marriages longer than five years and consider only two factors.

1. The duration of the marriage (rounded to the nearest whole number)
2. The incomes of the spouses at the time of dissolution (rounded to the nearest dollar)

To determine the amount of maintenance, we take the paying spouse's income and subtract the receiving spouse's income to get to the amount of spousal maintenance.

To determine the duration the maintenance will last, we take the number of years the parties were married and multiply by .015 - .5.

An indefinite maintenance award is appropriate if the marriage was longer than 20 years and the receiving spouse is over 50 years old.

Examples of the Guidelines

Example 1.

Herb and Wendy have been married for 20 years. Herb works as an attorney and earns $100k per year. Wendy works part-time for the school district and earns $20k per year. Herb is 42 and Wendy is 40.

Step 1. To determine the duration we take 20 x .15, or .30.

Step 2. Then we take Herb's monthly income and subtract Wendy's. $8333 - $1666 = $6666 (this represents the difference between Herb and Wendy's month- ly income).

Step 3. We then take $6666 and multiply it by .30 = $1999.80 monthly spousal maintenance.

Step 4. To determine how long Herb will pay Wendy $1999, we take the 20-year marriage and multiply it by anywhere between .3 - .5 – meaning the duration should be between 6 and 10 years of maintenance.

Example 2.

Harry and Wanda both work for Walmart. Harry works as a full-time cashier and Wanda works part-time in the salon. They have been married for 30 years and are both in their 60s. Harry earns $3500 per month and Wanda earns $1250.

Right off the bat, we know that the duration of support will be indefinite, because the length of marriage is over 20 years and the parties are over the age of 50.

Step 1. 0.15 x 30 = .45 (this is our multiplier)

Step 2. $3500 - $1250 = $2250

Step 3. $2250 x .45 = $1013

Step 4. Indefinite award.

Spousal Maintenance Modifications

Spousal maintenance awards are modifiable unless the order specifically states that the award is non-modifiable or the parties agree that the maintenance is not modifiable.

(However, a court cannot modify spousal maintenance unless an original order contained an award of spousal maintenance.)

A spouse seeking a modification must prove a "substantial and continuing change of circumstances affecting the purposes of the original decree" that requires the amount or duration of spousal maintenance to be modified.

For instance, in the event that the doctor ordered to pay spousal maintenance indefinitely (the one who hid assets and underperformed in his business) wants to terminate spousal maintenance payments, the burden will be on him to show the change in circumstances that is so substantial it will allow for the modification.

By contrast, if the wife has been awarded five years of maintenance in order to get her nursing degree, licensure and find employment, she will have the burden of proving a substantial change sufficient to warrant extending the maintenance. An injury, for instance, making it impossible for her to become a nurse, may be a sufficient change to extend the maintenance payments. This type of spousal maintenance award is called "rehabilitative," because it seeks to allow a spouse to become self-sufficient. Case law states it would be proper to modify an award if the circum- stances contemplated during the original order are not actually fulfilled. If a spouse exhibits "maximum good faith efforts" and still cannot become employed, the court can and has extended spousal maintenance durations.

Maintenance awards cannot be retroactively modified. This means that you must file to modify if a substantial change has occurred. The court cannot go back and change awards prior to the filing of the Petition to Modify.

Unless there is very specific language to the contrary, spousal maintenance ends upon the death of either party or the remarriage of the receiving spouse. However, the court of appeals ruled that cohabitation is not grounds for modifying spousal maintenance. That means even if your ex is now shacking up with a millionaire, that alone will not be grounds for modifying or terminating support. In one case, the court held that a wife's relationship with a third person was irrelevant and non- discoverable in a modification of maintenance case. By the same token, a husband's increase in income cannot justify a modification of maintenance. An ex-spouse cannot reasonably expect to reap the rewards of further accumulation of wealth after divorce.

Retirement may or may not be grounds for modification of an award. The question will be whether or not the retirement was contemplated at the time of the entry of the decree. In one case, a wife was awarded property in the divorce and the husband was ordered to pay the debts associated with the property. The court of appeals said the trial court judge could use the husband's non-payment of the debt as a change in circumstances warranting a change in spousal maintenance.

Spousal Maintenance Enforcement

Judgments for spousal maintenance are not the same as judgments for other debts. They are taken very seriously by the legislature and are non-dischargeable in bank- ruptcy. If a spouse isn't paying court-ordered maintenance, you do have options.

For example, the court can place a lien on the property of the spouse who isn't making the required maintenance payments. Other ways that maintenance can be enforced include: seizing the tax returns of a spouse who fails to pay maintenance, collecting through an income withholding order, or levying against a bank account. In one case, we were able to secure the funds of a personal injury claim to satisfy unpaid spousal maintenance.

The deadline to request a judgment for unpaid support is three years after the order has terminated. After you have secured your judgment, you need not renew it. The judgment will remain in full force and effect, in fact, failure to pay the judgment is a class 1 misdemeanor!

In order to create a lien you must:

1. Record the judgment,
2. File the lien by DES, or
3. The court can assign a specific security interest for the support payments.

In the event that your ex owes you unpaid spousal maintenance, you can file a peti- tion to enforce your decree. This may need to be filed in civil court depending on the decree, so check with an attorney prior to filing.

Taxes and Spousal Maintenance – This is important!

Many people fight paying spousal maintenance due to a stigma or sense of principle, and fail to realize the tax consequences associated with maintenance can be very valuable!

Alimony—per the Internal Revenue Service (IRS)—is taxable to the recipient and deductible by the paying spouse. This means every dollar you pay in spousal maintenance is money for which you do not owe taxes! This could lower your tax bracket significantly and it means that each dollar you pay is actually costing you closer to 70 cents. When used strategically, alimony can benefit both spouses.

Even though Arizona calls alimony "spousal maintenance," the IRS nevertheless treats it as alimony. It is an "above the line" deduction, which means it is an avail- able deduction even if the paying spouse does not itemize deductions. The spouse receiving maintenance must give his or her Social Security number to the paying spouse, who must list the Social Security number on the tax return.

For tax purposes, there are seven conditions for a payment to be alimony (or sepa- rate maintenance):

1. The payment must be in cash (not property or goods).
2. The payment must be received by (or on behalf of) a spouse under a divorce or separation agreement.
3. The payment must not be designated in the divorce or separation instrument as not includible in gross income or not allowable as a deduction.
4. If legally separated by a decree of divorce or separate maintenance, the spouses must not be members of the same household at the time of payment.
5. There is no liability to make any payment as substitute payment after the pay- ee's death and the instrument so states.
6. The payment is not in whole or in part for child support under the terms of the divorce or separation agreement.

7. The payment is not subject to recapture pursuant to <u>I.R.C. § 71(f).</u>

As you can see, spousal maintenance is a complex subject that is very difficult to navigate unless you have extensive knowledge in this area. If you are counting on spousal maintenance for part or all of your support after your marital dissolution— or if you are the spouse expected to pay maintenance to your ex—this is the most crucial time to seek the advice of a skilled, experienced attorney who is committed to fighting for your interests.

Notes

Chapter 12
Property

In any divorce case, all property is subject to division, meaning it must be identified, classified, and then divided.

Here, the principles of community property and community debt run parallel to one another, so as we talk about principles of community property, they can likely be applied to questions regarding whether or not debts are community or separate.

Identify all of the property in the possession of either spouse

There are several tools, rules, and statutes that help us identify all of the property a couple may have, including the required affidavit of financial information and the rule 49 disclosures required under the family law rules of procedure.

Many times, a couple may have bank accounts, retirement accounts, real property, time shares, vehicles, HSA accounts, businesses, jewelry, furniture, securities or in- vestments, and more.

If a spouse is being less than forthcoming regarding the property they have, your attorney may use interrogatories, request for production of documents, subpoenas, request for admissions, and/or depositions to help identify property. Sometimes a private investigator or a forensic accountant is used to help find property. For more on finding hidden assets, click here.

Classify all of the property as community, separate, or quasi-community

Community Property

In general, property acquired during your marriage is community property, regard- less of how your property is titled. This means that even if your husband's name is the only one on the loan and the title for the car he purchased a few years back, it is still considered community property.

Likewise, if your wife started a business five years ago while you were married and you have never had anything to do with the business, and you are not a member listed on the LLC, it is nevertheless community property.

In order to have community property, parties must have a valid marriage and the parties must be living in a community property state. This means that couples who are cohabitating, even for long periods of time, will not have accumulated community property.

For couples who have lived in both the community property state and separate property states, this could be particularly confusing. The general rule is that *the character of the property (separate or community) is determined by the laws of the state where the property was accumulated.*

Separate Property

Property each spouse owned before marriage, or acquired after the filing for separation that led to a divorce, is separate property. Property that was acquired by gift, bequest, or inheritance through intestacy (your wealthy great-granduncle died without a will) is separate property, even if it occurred during the marriage.

Sometimes this can be very tricky, especially when assets that were once separate become comingled or retitled during the marriage. It is also important to leave the door open in your petitions to account for the fact that spouses may have separate property either from before the marriage or from gifts or inheritance.

Exceptions to the rule

Separate property and community debt are as intricate as a spider web. Pre-nuptial agreements may have clauses allowing separate property or debts to be treated as community property. Once the spouses decide to end their marriage, they are free to negotiate a settlement, dividing the property and paying off debts. In other words, the parties can change the statutory rules by contract, as long as the contract is fair and reasonable.

Community property can be used to pay a separate debt incurred before the marriage, as long as it was incurred after September 1, 1973. It does set up a limitation—the community property will only pay a certain amount—the percent of the debt that would be deemed separate property if the spouse were single. That means the spouse who incurred a debt only gets a partial settlement from community property. The debtor will have to look for other ways to collect the remaining amount.

Generally, debts entered into before the marriage remain the separate property of each spouse, and do not form part of the marital community. Creditors are unable to reach one party's separate property in order to pay the other's separate debt. That is why it is so important that Arizona residents know the nature of their assets and debts before filing a petition for separation. Ideally there is full communication and disclosure between the spouses, because assumptions and misunderstandings will only lead to financial problems.

Division Upon Divorce

The general rule is that all of the property is subject to equitable division. Equitable division means there is a presumption for a 50/50 split of the entire community or marital estate. This presumption can be rebutted in instances of marital waste or other facts that make "equitable distribution" something other than 50% to each spouse. For more information on community waste, check out the section on spousal maintenance.

All property must be divided upon divorce. It is very important that we identify and divide all property. Otherwise, it is owned by both parties as tenants in common.

Property division is NON-MODIFIABLE. This means that if you enter into an agreement or a judge enters an order for property division, you cannot go back and ask for a reallocation of those assets (with several exceptions). It is therefore extremely important to do your due diligence in researching your assets and their value, and to present your property information clearly and concisely to the judge.

Quasi-Community Property

Property a couple acquired while living in a non-community property state, before moving to Arizona, is referred to as quasi-community property. The Arizona Legislature created the quasi-community property rule officially in 1973:

> "property acquired by either spouse outside the state shall be deemed to be community property if said property would have been community property if acquired in this state[.]"

This means that in the event you seek a divorce in Arizona, Arizona court will treat the property you accumulated out of state as community property. The big exception here is with regards to partnership interests, which are treated as personal property governed by the laws of the state where a married couple lived when the partnership interests were acquired.

If land or real estate is acquired during marriage, it is presumed to be community property. The spouse seeking to claim that it is a separate property has the burden of proving by clear and convincing evidence that the property is in fact separate. If the property benefits the community—for example, the parties live in the home, rent out the home and enjoy the proceeds together, or vacation together in the home every summer—it is strongly presumed that the debt acquired to finance the trans- action is community debt.

Community property is subject to "equitable division." Equitable division means the property will be divided essentially equally. This doesn't mean that each asset must be split down the middle, but that the final split must be essentially equal unless there is a specific reason why an equal split isn't "equitable."

Property division must be substantially equal in the absence of compelling factors

This means that unless a judge makes a specific finding of "compelling factors," property must be divided substantially equally. This is where your constitutional right to life, liberty and property actually shows up. If the court fails to divide your property substantially equally, you have been deprived of your vested right to your property.

If the parties don't agree on how to divide the community property, the court will ask both husband and wife to present a plan for how to divide the properties and debts.

Separate Property

All property owned prior to marriage is the separate property of that spouse, and it continues to stay the separate property that spouse, as long as no action is taken to change the character of the property. The timing of acquiring the property and not necessarily the title controls. Even if the car or house is titled in the name of one spouse, it will be treated as community property if acquired during the marriage.

Additionally, any property that a spouse receives as a gift or inheritance is also separate property, even after the marriage.

Any interest, rents, or profits from separate property earned during the marriage will remain separate property, and subsequent purchases or acquisitions will also remain separate property.

Other forms of separate property will be discussed at length below and include:

- Social Security retirement benefits
- Professional degrees
- Personal Injury Damages for Pain and Suffering
- Some Irrevocable Trust contributions

Co-mingled Property

The general rule is that separate property or debts remain separate unless there is clear transmutation or comingling of the funds. The main test of whether or not property or an asset has become community is determined by the intent of the owning spouse. For instance, if separate funds are used to purchase a home that is then titled in both the husband's and wife's names as joint tenants, the property has likely been gifted to the community or "transmuted."

In another case, a home owned by the husband and used as the marital home remained the separate property of the husband, even when the mortgage was paid with community funds. In that case, if community funds have been used to improve the separate property of one spouse, the community may have a "lien" or be owed money from the separate spouse.

These cases are extremely fact-sensitive. That means that whether the court will consider property transmuted will be determined based on what actually happened. If Wife helped build and grow Husband's separate business, the court is more likely to award Wife an interest in the business. If Husband helped to remodel Wife's apartment complex, Husband will likely have an interest in the apartment complex or rents, even if the property is Wife's separate property.

This is often overlooked by the spouse who could be owed funds! It is most certainly worth speaking with an attorney if you have questions on transmutation, comingling or community liens.

The Court of Appeals issues the following formula to help determine what the community portion is of an asset that is both separate and community property, or separate property where a community lien exists.

Specifically, where "A" = appreciation of the property during the marriage, where "B" = the appraised value of the property as of the date of the marriage, and where "C" = the community's contributions to principal, the value of the community's lien is: $C + [C/B \quad x A]$.

Check out the Modern Law Website to use *our prebuilt calculator* www.mymodernlaw.com

Land/ Real Estate

Land can be community or separate property, depending on when the land was purchased or acquired and whether or not funds used to purchase the land are separate funds or community funds. The increase in value may or may not be community assets. See the discussion on comingling above.

Professional Businesses

The business will be broken down into its component parts or assets. Each asset will then be evaluated to determine whether or not it is community property.

Assets most often include:

- The professional degree
- The license to practice
- The building
- Bank accounts
- Inventory/ physical assets
- Accounts receivable
- Goodwill

The degree and license to practice in a professional business will always be separate property, but the other assets will be evaluated based on when and how they were acquired. Most interestingly, the accounts receivable may be valued without regards to taxes and overhead expenses. In Arizona, professional goodwill is valued as a community asset.

Let's take an example. Dr. Bill Thomas owns a dental practice. His wife Katherine helped put him through dental school and has supported him for the duration of their 20-year marriage. She never worked in the practice, but stayed home with their 4 children. Dr. Thomas received a loan from his father to start the practice, and has paid off all but $10,000 of the $100,000 loan. The business has about $1million in annual revenue, $75,000 in accounts receivable and about 1,500 annual patients. Katherine wants to know what her interest in the business might be worth.

First, we would identify the pieces of the business.

The degree and license to practice are property of the business, but separate property of Dr. Thomas. A professional degree like a degree to practice law, dentistry, medicine, accounting, etc. is the separate property of the spouse who earned the degree, regardless of whether or not the degree was earned during the marriage or if the other spouse paid for the education. So, even though Katherine supported Bill through dental school, she has no claim to his dental license or degree.

The physical assets including the dental chairs, tools, x-ray machines, etc. are all community property because they were acquired during the marriage. The accounts receivable total $75,000. The entire balance will likely qualify as community property subject to division.

Goodwill is the reputation value of the business. It's not cash, but it is the value that comes from the excess income, stream of customers, reputation of the business and the practitioner (Dr. Thomas), etc. Business goodwill is community property in Arizona and subject to equitable division.

When businesses are involved, you will most likely need a business valuation. A licensed business valuator will assess the total value of the business and will be needed to establish the total value for trial or to mediate and settle your divorce amicably. Look for a licensed business appraiser and check out our resource list if you need recommendations.

Let's see what happens when we change the facts slightly. Let's say Dr. Thomas funded his dental practice entirely from an inheritance. The inheritance is separate property. The general rule is that interest and profits from separate property remain separate property. However, the other general rule is that wages earned during the marriage are community property.

In Arizona, income and profits created by the business itself, not the "toil and application" of the spouses, will be separate. Actual labor or profits from labor and marketing efforts of the spouse will be community. Therefore, Dr. Thomas will argue that his wages earned as a dentist, his salary, is community property, but the excess profits earned by the business are his separate property created from his investment of separate funds.

Here is where it is essential to have an experienced and talented lawyer working on your behalf. The burden is largely on the spouse who is claiming the assets are separate to prove, by clear and convincing evidence, which portion of the assets are separate and why. In the event they fail to meet their burden, the whole of the value and assets will be divided as community property.

Most often, it isn't practical or in anyone's interest for a closely held business to be sold with the proceeds divided. The most typical outcome is that one spouse is awarded the business in whole and the other spouse will be awarded offsetting assets or payments toward the balance owed for his or her interest in the business.

This can be very complicated, so here is another example. In one case, the Arizona court determined that the growth of the business due to inflation, increased demand and the efforts of others were the separate property of the husband, but growth attributable to community labor would be split as community property. In that case, the wife worked as an office manager in the business. As you can see, this is both factually sensitive and legally complex, but with proper planning and legal assistance, you can set yourself up for the best possible outcome.

Retirement Benefits/Stock Options

Retirement benefits include pensions, 401ks and profit sharing arrangements. They are part of a compensation plan earned during employment and are treated as community property if accumulated during the marriage. Retirement benefits earned before marriage or after the service of the petition for dissolution or legal separation are separate property of the spouse who earned them. This rule applies to both employer and employee contributions.

The tricky part comes when some portion of the retirement was earned pre-marriage, then comingled with post-marriage contributions. In that case, the court can use the following formula to determine the community portion at the asset or the value of the community lien:

Specifically, where "A" = appreciation of the property during the marriage, where "B" = the appraised value of the property as of the date of the marriage, and where "C" = the community's contributions to principal, the value of the com- munity's lien is: $C + [C/B \times A]$.

In certain situations, a disabled spouse is given the option of selecting disability benefits instead of retirement benefits. In the event the spouse selects disability benefits to the exclusion of the retirement benefits, each spouse will be given the community interest in the disability benefits. The disability benefits will only be divisible in divorce action when they're selected in lieu of retirement funds.

After a retirement benefit is awarded to a spouse in a divorce, it immediately becomes the vested property of the spouse it was awarded to. Most often, a qualified domestic relations order, or QDRO, is required to divide the qualified retirement accounts.

Non-vested benefits may also be subject to division, although the court needs to take into account the fact that those interests may disappear due to no fault of either spouse. The court is likely best served by dividing the non-vested benefits at the time of dissolution, allowing them to grow separately and equally, as opposed to offsetting non-vested benefits with vested benefits.

In divorce proceedings, if the trial court determines that the employer's intent in granting the husband unvested stock options was to compensate him for past or current service, the stock options would be community property and allocated between the parties under the appropriate time rule formula. However, if the intent of the employer was to provide an incentive for the husband's future performance, it would be assumed that the period of employment prior to the granting of the options did not contribute to the husband earning the stock options and thus should not be included in the time used to calculate the community's interest in the options.

An interest in vested retirement accounts could result in a lump sum payout, an offset of the other community interests, or a payment and monthly installments over time.

The court has stated a general preference, when possible, to leave retirement accounts untouched, and to offset a spouse's interest in retirement assets with other community interests. Vested pension rights are those not subject to forfeiture if employment is terminated and matured rights are unconditional rights to immediate payment.

That opinion further said that vested and non-vested rights may be community property subject to equitable division and that a non-employee spouse may be awarded her community interest under:

1. The present cash value method, or
2. The reserved jurisdiction method.

Social Security

Congress has created specific language stating that Social Security benefits are the separate property of the person receiving the benefits. That means Social Security payments will not be divided as community property. It's important to note that even non-working spouses may have their own separate Social Security benefits, which will be the sole property of the receiving spouse.

Remember that Social Security is counted as "income" and can be garnished for the payment of child support or spousal maintenance.

Disability Benefits

Disability benefits are in place to replace the earnings that one would receive if one were working; they are not in place to compensate the disabled spouse for pain and suffering. Therefore, payments received during the marriage are community property subject to division. Payments received after the divorce (or service of the petition for divorce) will be the separate property of the disabled spouse, even though the injury may have occurred during the marriage.

This can be contrasted with how the court treats retirement benefits. The purpose of retirement benefits is to "defer compensation" for later living expenses. This is why retirement money received after the marriage, is treated as community property and disability proceeds received after the marriage is treated as separate property.

In other words, the community does not acquire a right to future disability payouts once the community ends.

Insurance Proceeds

The renewal value of insurance policies may be a community asset that needs to be identified, valued and divided.

Life Insurance Policies:

The value of a life insurance policy on dissolution of marriage is its cash surrender value. A former wife who is the designated beneficiary of her ex-husband's life insurance is entitled to the proceeds when the rights have not been terminated by agreement or divorce decree.

National Serviceman's Life Insurance proceeds are governed by federal policy; thus the service person who owns the policy can determine the beneficiary regardless of the community source of the funds used to pay the   premiums.

Family Law Master:

When cases involve complicated issues surrounding stocks, deferred compensation, retirement benefits, or other tricky financial matters, a family law master can be appointed to offer the court information related to these financial matters.

Undivided Property

§ 25–318(B), provides that community property not disposed of in a dissolution decree is thereafter owned by the former spouses as tenants in common.

The second statute, A.R.S. § 14–2804, provides that a divorce automatically rescinds any pre-dissolution revocable disposition or appointment of property made by a divorced spouse to that person's former spouse.

Military Benefits

Military retirement benefits are community property. Congress actually passed an act to protect military spouses and make certain they could receive a portion of the retirement benefits earned during their marriage to their spouses.

Gifts

A gift from one spouse of separate property to the other spouse will convert that property into the separate property of the receiving spouse. This can be tricky, because the spouse receiving property must prove that the property transfer was intended to be a gift. For instance, if a husband sells his land in Iowa that he owned before the marriage and buys his wife expensive jewelry, that jewelry may be the separate property of the wife, if she can establish that the husband intended to give her a gift and not to convert the asset to a community investment of jewelry. Instead, if Husband sold his land in Iowa and then purchased a beach home, titled in both Husband and Wife's name, Wife could argue that Husband gifted the home to the community. If she could establish his donative intent, the property would likely be community and subject to division.

To establish a gift has been made, you must prove "donative intent." That means you will need to show that the money or land was given as a gift and not a loan or repayment.

Notes

Conclusion

Now that you've reached the end of this book, I hope that you have some of the answers to the perplexing questions that can arise during this very emotional transition. Remember that every situation is different and every family dynamic will have individual problems, and varying solutions for addressing those challenges. As stated in the beginning, this book wasn't meant to be a step-by-step "how-to" for filing a divorce, but more of a guide to make sure you are asking all the right questions, and considering every aspect of your case.

By now, you should have some idea as to how you wish to proceed and what your options are. I would always advise individuals to seek professional representation, but I also realize that isn't always possible. This book should help you accurately assess your position, and to help you get started in selecting an attorney should you choose to seek representation. Use it as a reference whenever questions arise, and to help you stay organized.

Remember that the main goal is for you to best be able to represent yourself and your interests, and if any of the information contained in this book will help you do that, then I'm glad I could help.

—Billie Tarascio

*** **Disclaimer******

This book is not a substitute for legal advice and reading the book does not create an attorney client relationship or any of the benefits and privileges that comes from working with an attorney. The book is provided for informational purposes only and does not constitute legal advice.

CPSIA information can be obtained
at www.ICGtesting.com
Printed in the USA
FFHW011947151019
55593505-61406FF